CONTEMPORARY
LITERATURE

Louis de Bernières

SERIES EDITORS
Jonathan Noakes
and
Margaret Reynolds

Also available in Vintage Living Texts

Margaret Atwood
Focusing on
The Handmaid's Tale
The Blind Assassin
Bluebeard's Egg and Other Stories

Sebastian Faulks
Focusing on
Birdsong
Charlotte Gray
The Girl at the Lion d'Or

Ian McEwan
Focusing on
The Child in Time
Enduring Love
Atonement

VINTAGE
LIVING
TEXTS

Louis de Bernières

THE ESSENTIAL GUIDE
TO CONTEMPORARY
LITERATURE

Captain Corelli's Mandolin

The War of Don Emmanuel's Nether Parts

Señor Vivo and the Coca Lord

The Troublesome Offspring of Cardinal Guzman

V

VINTAGE

Published by Vintage 2002

2 4 6 8 10 9 7 5 3 1

First published in Great Britain in 2002 by Vintage

Random House, 20 Vauxhall Bridge Road,
London SW1V 2SA

Random House Australia (Pty) Limited
20 Alfred Street, Milsons Point, Sydney,
New South Wales 2061, Australia

Random House New Zealand Limited
18 Poland Road, Glenfield,
Auckland 10, New Zealand

Random House (Pty) Limited
Endulini, 5A Jubilee Road, Parktown 2193, South Africa

The Random House Group Limited Reg. No. 954009
www.randomhouse.co.uk

A CIP catalogue record for this book is available from the British Library

ISBN 0099437570

Papers used by Random House are natural, recyclable products made from wood grown in sustainable forests; the manufacturing processes conform to the environmental regulations of the country of origin.

Typeset by Palimpsest Book Production Limited, Polmont, Stirlingshire

Printed and bound in Great Britain by
Bookmarque Ltd, Croydon, Surrey   OCT 23 2003

CONTENTS

VINTAGE LIVING TEXTS: PREFACE

LOUIS DE BERNIÈRES

VINTAGE LIVING TEXTS

Captain Corelli's Mandolin

The War of Don Emmanuel's Nether Parts

Señor Vivo and the Coca Lord

The Troublesome Offspring of Cardinal Guzman

VINTAGE LIVING TEXTS: REFERENCE

Acknowledgements

We owe grateful thanks to all at Random House. Most of all our debt is to Caroline Michel and her team at Vintage – especially Marcella Edwards – who have given us generous and unfailing support. Thanks also to Philippa Brewster and Georgina Capel, Michael Meredith, Angela Leighton, Harriet Marland, Louisa Joyner, Zara Warshal, to all our colleagues, and to our partners and families. We would also like to thank the teachers and students at schools and colleges around the country who have taken part in our trialling process, and who have responded so readily and warmly to our requests for advice. And finally, our thanks to Louis de Bernières for his work without whom . . . without which . . .

VINTAGE LIVING TEXTS

Preface

About this series

Vintage Living Texts: The Essential Guide to Contemporary Literature is a new concept in reading guides. Our aim is to provide readers of all kinds with an intelligent and accessible introduction to key works of contemporary literature. Each guide suggests techniques for reading important contemporary novels, and offers a variety of back-up materials that will give you ways into the text – without ever telling you what to think.

Content

All the books reproduce an extensive interview with the author, conducted exclusively for this series. This is not to say that we believe that the author's word is law. Of course it isn't. Once his or her book has gone out into the world he or she becomes simply yet another – if singularly competent – reader. This series recognises that an author's contribution may be valuable, and intriguing, but it puts the reader in control.

Every title in the series is author-focused and covers at

least three of their novels, along with relevant biographical, bibliographical, contextual and comparative material.

How to use this series

In the reading activities that make up the core of each book you will see that you are asked to do two things. One comes from the text; that is, we suggest what you should focus on, whether it's a theme, the language or the narrative method. The other concentrates on your own response. We want you to think about how you are reading, and what skills you are bringing to bear in doing that reading. So this part is very much about you, the reader.

The point is that there are many ways of responding to a text. You could concentrate on the methods you might use to compare this text with others. In that case, look for the sections headed 'Compare'. Or you might want to do something more individual, and analyse how you are reacting to a text and what it means to you, in which case, pick out the approaches labelled 'Imagine' or 'Ask Yourself'.

Of course, it may well be that you are reading these texts for an exam. In that case you will have to go for the more traditional methods of literary criticism and look for the responses that tell you to 'Discuss' or 'Analyse'. Whichever level you (or your students) are at, you will find that there is something here for everyone. However, we're not suggesting that you stick solely to the approaches we offer, nor that you tackle all of the exercises laid out here. Choose whatever most interests you, or whatever best suits your purposes.

Who are these books for?

Students will find that these guides are like a good teacher. They introduce the life and work of the author, set each novel in its context, explain key ideas and literary critical terms as they arise, suggest comparative exercises in a number of media, and ask focused questions to encourage a well-informed, analytical approach to reading the novels in a way that is rigorous, but still entertaining.

Teachers will find in this series a rich source of ideas for teaching contemporary novels and their contexts, particularly at AS, A and undergraduate level. The exercises on each text have been tailored to meet the various assessment objectives laid down in the subject criteria for GCE AS and GCE A Level English Literature, and are explained in such a way that they can easily be selected and fitted into a lesson plan. Given the diversity of ways in which the awarding bodies have devised their specifications to meet these assessment objectives, a wide range of exercises is offered. We've had fun devising the plans, and we hope that they'll be fun for you when you come to teach and learn with them.

And if you are neither a teacher nor a student of contemporary literature, but someone reading for your own pleasure? Well, if you've ever wanted someone to introduce you to a novelist's work in a way that will let you trust your own judgement and read more confidently, then this guide is also for you.

Whoever you are, we hope that you will enjoy using these books and that they will send you back to the novels to find new pleasures.

All page references in this text refer to the Vintage edition.

Louis de Bernières

Introduction

At the end of *Captain Corelli's Mandolin* Iannis persuades
Velisarios the strong man to lift the huge stone that covers the
cachette in the ruins of what once was the doctor's house. He
is looking for the mandolin which his grandmother Pelagia has
said was hidden there, long ago. Velisarios has come to the
house to fulfil a private ritual, placing a red rose on the grave
of a long dead Italian soldier. He obliges Iannis and Spiro by
displaying his legendary strength and raises the lid of the
cachette: 'Did you know', says Iannis, 'that Cephallonia was
the original place where the giants lived? It says so in Homer.
That's what Grandma says.'

In these references – to Pelagia, to Velisarios, to Carlo, to
the mandolin – we have the whole story of *Captain Corelli's
Mandolin*. As we have it again in the treasures unearthed from
the cachette: the wind-up gramophone, the crocheted wedding
blanket, the bandoliers of bullets, the two manuscripts, one in
Italian and one in Cyrillic, the Lee-Enfield rifle, and the mandolin. The contents of the cachette are a mnemonic. And
because we have lived through the story, each fragment is
weighted with a meaning that we understand. But the story we
remember is itself a mnemonic for Greek history, for Greek

legend, literature and myth, for the significance of Greek civilisation and its place in European memory and in the memory
of the world.

Louis de Bernières likes a big canvas. That may be a strange
thing to say about a book set largely on an island. But islands
in literature are often magic boxes. In the *Odyssey* of Homer
each of the islands Ulysses visits presents him with new
wonders, but also with new challenges that teach him about
himself, whether it's the seductions of Circe's sophistication
set against the simplicity of Nausicca's innocence, or the depre-
dations of the Cyclops countered by a wiliness that exploits
the monster's weakness, or the deadly pleasure of the Sirens
song, attended to, but overcome through the discipline of a
planned restraint. Homer's islands were among the first in
literature to be used to tell that story of how you find out
about who you are – not at home, but by going away from
home. After that, there was Prospero's island in Shakespeare's
The Tempest, there was Robinson Crusoe's island in Daniel
Defoe's eponymous novel, there was R. M. Ballantyne's *Coral
Island*, and Robert Louis Stevenson's *Treasure Island* and the
unnamed island inhabited by Piggy and Ralph and all the other
lost boys in William Golding's *The Lord of the Flies*.

Captain Corelli's Mandolin might look like a focussed story
about one woman and her life in one place across a huge span
of time. But look again. Pelagia is the centre of the novel, but
the derivation of her name refers to a particular ocean current.
Through the current of Pelagia's story run all those earlier
stories set on islands, and, like them, this one is not so much
about an individual person as it is about society and commu-
nication between people and the accidents of history that
destroy those relations between people. It is a big canvas. And
that's one reason why de Bernières likes to give himself a lot
of space. The main action of *Captain Corelli* may take place
over a few years, but the larger frame is the whole of Pelagia's

and Corelli's long lives. Interestingly, in the 2001 film adaptation with a screenplay by Shawn Slovo, the decision was made to shorten the time span, so Corelli returns fairly soon after the war. It makes a 'happier' ending perhaps, but it also makes a tidier one. The doctor is still alive, the joke about the pea in Stammatis's ear takes us back to the beginning. Of course it's easy to see why the filmmakers did this, just as it's easy to see why Pelagia – in the film – has to be allowed to qualify as a real doctor. But there is something too neat about this resolution that is entirely contrary to de Bernières's sprawling, fragmentary method. This is, after all, the writer who – as he tells us in the interview – had originally intended his Latin American trilogy to go on to extend to five books.

There is an organic quality to de Bernières's writing and three factors contribute to that. He prefers – as he explains – a first person narrative, but even when he uses the third person, the narrating voice has a personality that is distinctively ironic, dry, half amused, half shocked by the perversities of human behaviour. The use of this voice and the individual voices of the characters often make his works sound like a chorus or a range of dialogues rather than a novel. The episodic structure of his style is the second element that creates the organic character of his work. It is almost an haphazard process. De Bernières writes the individual chapters, then decides on their order: the novel happens as it grows. The third feature is de Bernières's typical slides between a realist mode and a magical, fantasy world. This is more obvious in the Latin American trilogy, but it's true too of *Captain Corelli's Mandolin*, even if there it is used for different – perhaps more serious – purposes. In Chapter 19, 'L'Omosessuale (6)', for instance – two worlds jostle each other as Carlo tells a made up story of heroism and glory to Francesco's mother, even as he recalls the sordid truth of Francesco's last hours.

Louis de Bernières is a story teller. That's why he likes to

7

re-tell other stories: Homer's *Odyssey* is behind *Captain Corelli's Mandolin*; the Exodus from Egypt and the journey to the Promised Land from the Bible is behind the Latin American trilogy. Then there are his own stories in the shapes of his novels. Antonio Corelli's mandolin is called Antonia, because it is the female part of himself; the strings of the mandolin stitch his wounds and stay in his body for the rest of his life; Pelagia's foundling child is named Antonia, and it is the fact of her presence that keeps Antonio away for so many years. It's just one small story within his many larger stories, but it grows, as his novels grow, as all his stories grow.

In de Bernières's own introduction to the published version of his radio play *Sunday Morning at the Centre of the World* (2001) he speaks of how the work happened. It came, he says, out of a particular experience of living and working in Earlsfield in South West London. But then he says that everything that happened to him – and led to the play – was accidental, contingent, unplanned. He lost the job he'd gone there for, he acquired a cat, he started to write. We don't have to believe in this literally of course – it is, as much as anything, another one of his stories. But then he says, 'There is in fact almost nothing fictional in the anecdotes and stories told here, and all the voices have their real counterparts'. Like so much of his work, *Sunday Morning at the Centre of the World* comes out of listening to real voices, then letting those voices speak for themselves so that they take the story wherever it goes, and the story itself takes the lead.

It is for this reason that de Bernières's stories don't really end. They come to a resolution certainly, but there's a sense of there being yet another story just beyond, just around the corner, still to be told. Parlanchina beckons at the end of *The War of Don Emmanuel's Nether Parts*, the vision of three girls on a moped seduces at the end of *Captain Corelli's Mandolin*. The novel stops, but the story carries on.

Interview with Louis de Bernières

Norfolk: 4 September 2001

CAPTAIN CORELLI'S MANDOLIN

MR: Why did the moment come when you changed your scene from an imaginary South America to Greece?

LdeB: I was going to do five Latin-American books, including one about a dictator. But by the time that came along, Latin America had democratised completely, apart from Cuba, so the book would have been out of date – there was no one left. The Argentine junta had gone, Pinochet had gone from Chile, and Noriega had gone; there was really no one left apart from Castro. So that would have become an anachronism. And the other thing was that by the end of the third novel I realised that I was spending much too much time recapitulating what happened in the first two novels in case the reader hadn't read them. And I thought, my God, if I get to number five, it'll be entirely about what happened in the other books. And so I just stopped. In the meantime, I had written a novel about Yugoslavia which hasn't been published, so I wasn't in any case all the time in South America. And then I had a girlfriend at the time who was really sick of going on summer holiday to France all the time.

We used to take my Morris Minor over the Channel and drive around France. She said, 'Please can we go somewhere else?' So I said, 'OK, you arrange the holiday,' and she choose Greece and this particular island, and when we went there the story of Captain Corelli just fell into my lap.

MR: How? The idea just came to you?

LdeB: Well, as soon as you get into the tourist coach, the tourist guide says, 'After the earthquake in 1953,' and you think, 'What earthquake? I haven't heard of this.' That's what got me interested. And then I heard stories about the Italian occupation and the massacres by the Nazis, and I heard that the Greeks and the Italians on the island had got on reasonably well, so it seemed an obvious idea really to have a romance across the national boundary lines.

MR: You mention the earthquake, the occupation and the massacres. Did you do a lot of research for this?

LdeB: I did. Much of that holiday was taken up with riding around on a motorbike, getting the feel of the place and spotting things, and when I got home I wrote to the librarian of the cultural and historical museum in Argostoli, which is the capital of Cephallonia, and she sent me a reading list, and really, it all started from there. And then fortunate things happened, such as a man turning up at my neighbour's who'd been in the earthquake. I had to write to the Greek ambassador and all sorts to get information. It's amazing what you have to try and find out. I mean, when was the Orthodox Easter Day in 1943 – that kind of thing. I just did masses of reading and masses of talking to people. Much of the book is based on *The Odyssey* – it's absolutely stuffed with references to Homer – that's just a clue for readers.

MR: I was intrigued by all the allusions to the Greek legends. You do it incredibly lightly. But you just sew them in as little allusions, don't you, and leave it at that?

LdeB: Well, sewing is a good word because, for example, Pelagia is trying to sew a waistcoat or a wedding blanket or something which she keeps unpicking – just like Penelope, waiting for Odysseus to come back.

MR: Of course the Greek legends aren't the only set of allusions you use. There are the songs, the poems, the philosophical writers like Bertrand Russell that keep coming in – so you just feel that this is a body of reference that you can use and resort to all the time?

LdeB: I think because I have so many and so diverse interests, and I've travelled a lot and picked up bits and pieces from all over the place, I've got a large, but rather weird bank to draw on.

MR: Obviously, one of the things that you are drawing on in *Captain Corelli* is opera. What is your interest in opera?

LdeB: I'm not as interested in opera as you might think. My father loves opera. But it's just that if you have to find out about something, you do. You can't write a novel on an epic scale and expect to be lazy, you have to do the work. And it's a mistake to assume that everything that's in a book is actually connected with what the writer likes, or does. For example, Captain Corelli hates Wagner, right – and he tells his German friend that you get shot if you like Wagner. Actually, though, I do like Wagner. But when it comes to opera I'm really just the sort of person who likes listening to the highlights, you know, the choruses and the arias. I get very, very, very cheesed off with all the recitative.

MR: Something that struck me immediately at the beginning of *Captain Corelli* is the doctor's intriguing interest in long words. You like words, don't you, because in the Latin-American scenes we get all these different dialects and words from different languages.

LdeB: Well, Greek doctors are notorious for trying to impress you with long words and complicated explanations, so it was a joke about Greek doctors. For some reason, a lot of them are interested in history as well. It is true that I am very enamoured of language in general. It's something I get a great deal from Latin-American writers. Some one like Gabriel García Márquez is happy to use words like 'prodigious', you know *'marvillosa'*, lovely words, and I'm rather the same. I don't belong to that Anglo-Saxon and American school of writing where it's very simple and very clear, which I associate with Hemingway. You know. 'He stood up. He left.' I like to sort of wallow . . .

MR: And you're drawing on lots of different languages in order to do that.

LdeB: Yes, I do draw a lot on foreign languages, and I even invent words as well. There was a word in *Captain Corelli* which I invented, and I had a thank-you letter from a doctor afterwards. The word was 'iatric', meaning 'of or pertaining to a doctor'. It comes from the Greek *'iatros'*. Funnily enough, having invented it and published it and received thank-you letters from doctors, saying 'thank you for this word, which we needed', I then looked it up in the *Oxford English Dictionary* and it actually already existed. Which is sad, isn't it? There's a lovely Greek word *'megalopsiki'*, which means 'magnanimous'. And I would love to one day put that in a story – have somebody being 'megalopsical'. And let people puzzle that one out.

MR: Connected to this language question, there's a phrase, 'And thus it was that', or 'So it happened that', as though you are conscious of using a fairy-tale technique. Could you comment on that?

LdeB: Yes, my style is in many ways very old-fashioned. I grew up reading writers like Walter Scott. I am conscious of being part of this tradition of storytelling which goes back a long time, and I'm quite happy to use old-fashioned tropes. For example, just look at the long chapter headings – 'In which so and so does so and so and such a thing happens'. Which I think is fun, I like it. It's eighteenth century in flavour, like much of my narrating.

I feel very, very fortunate that I had to learn Latin from a very early age and so I have all the Latin grammatical constructions in my mind which of course people don't use any more, but I still remember them and they come to me perfectly naturally.

MR: And it actually gives you layers of tenses in your verbs then, doesn't it? Rather like the layers of resonance in your choice of characters' names in *Captain Corelli*.

LdeB: I often choose names for Kratylic reasons. Kratylus was an ancient Greek who thought that names were actually intimately connected with objects. That a table was called a table because it was a particularly tabley thing. So Pelagia, it means 'ocean', and a pelagic current is one that goes in a huge circle and comes back to where it starts, so that's why I chose the name for her.

MR: And Iannis, and Mandras?

LdeB: Iannis is just 'John' in Greek. And Mandras . . . I found that name in a novel and it's been very puzzling to Greeks because they'd never heard of it, but it certainly exists now!

MR: And you play with the Italian and the German names as well, such as Weber and Corelli.

LdeB: Of course, Corelli was a great composer. One of my favourites. And Weber is one of my favourite German composers.

MR: In *Captain Corelli*, perhaps more than in the other novels, there's a really strange mixture of you making jokes on the one hand, of actually being quite jesterish, and on the other being very sad, or very ironic, or painful. It's a personal question, but how much of that does come out of you?

LdeB: I think we're all rather like this. You know, you can be outrageously sad one morning because your loved one has left you, and then be laughing for a few minutes at some radio programme in the afternoon, and then feeling sad again when it's finished. We aren't particularly consistent, emotionally, it's one of the odd things about humans. And we're not rational creatures either, as Schopenhauer pointed out, we're really irrational creatures driven by strange motives and inclinations that even we don't really understand. So I think it's quite normal to have extremes of mood or temperament, as well as extremes of comedy or tragedy in a novel.

MR: Captain Corelli doesn't actually appear until page 188. Would you say something about that delay?

LdeB: The delay was simply because I was setting up the scene. *Captain Corelli* has a pyramidal structure. It has a very wide base, with lots and lots of characters, including Mussolini and the Greek dictator, and as the story progresses, it gets smaller and smaller and smaller, until it's at a little point. It's just Pelagia and Corelli at the end. So the whole thing is a triangle, and that meant that Corelli had to come in later, that's all. Really the book isn't about him anyway. It's about Pelagia and Dr Iannis.

MR: At the end, after the cache has been restored, I felt an enormous pleasure, as a reader, in thumbing through all those mementoes which actually we too had recognised. It's almost as though you've given the reader a memory. And you just list the mementoes. We don't need them explained, because we've been there. So that's one of the things that that pyramidal structure gives you, because there are so many things that we remember from the beginning. At the end, it's just Pelagia and Corelli, except that it opens out into that strange little vision of the three girls on the moped. Who are they?

LdeB: I've had interesting letters from people saying, 'Are they the three Fates?' and if you think about it . . . one of them's facing forward, looking to the future, one's reading the newspaper, and the other is facing backwards, so it's past, present and future. But the honest truth is this was something I actually saw in Corfu. I saw three really gorgeous young girls in white skirts, with suntanned thighs – all three of them on a moped doing exactly what I described there, and I thought it was so beautiful, and so cool, so typically Greek cool, that I just had to get it on paper somewhere. It seemed to me to sum up the spirit of Greece. It's sort of dangerous, but marvellous. And this is how I feel the Greeks are.

MR: And exciting and beautiful – and it's amazing how an image can convey all that, because in a way you don't have to say 'Who are they?' – it's there in the picture.

LdeB: And on the last page, Antonio Corelli looks at these girls and he feels a new piece of music coming, a Greek concerto, and so it's part of the hope that I think the book ought to leave you with. Not just the hope for Pelagia and Antonio, but the hope for new things coming out of even such an old man.

THE WAR OF DON EMMANUEL'S NETHER PARTS

SEÑOR VIVO AND THE COCA LORD

THE TROUBLESOME OFFSPRING OF CARDINAL GUZMAN

MR: Quite early in the *The War of Don Emmanuel's Nether Parts*, there's a little section where you start to describe the different layers of society and the different constituents of it, and who they are and where they function. Did this range of different caste levels give you a bigger canvas to work on? Did Latin America appeal to you from that point of view?

LdeB: I've noticed that I tend to put people from all walks of life into my novels, I don't seem to concentrate exclusively on one class or another, or on one type of person or another. When I was in Columbia I was living on a ranch, and mainly living with peasants, so I didn't have the chance to develop into the sort of north London type of writer who just writes about themselves and their friends having dinner parties. I like to include everybody, and by that I mean including animals and old people and children and all sorts, because they're all parts of our lives.

MR: How much of that experience of living in Columbia with peasants went into the book?

LdeB: Quite a lot of the characters are based on people I knew, or exaggerations, caricatures, or distortions of them. So there was a Pedro, for example, who was a hunter who had lots of dogs. There was a man called Michael who could cure cattle by whispering in their ears, and there was somebody called Hectoro who had a revolver and four wives. Although I never named the country in those books, many of the characters are based on people I knew.

MR: And how did you end up there in the first place?

LdeB: Well, that is a long story. It was to do with being expected to go into the army by my family. My family is one of those ones where you either go into the clergy or the military. It takes a long time for these traditions to die. I spent four months at Sandhurst trying to become an officer, and then went into the army and I realised that we were totally incompatible because I don't like giving orders, and I don't like being told what to do either. So it was hopeless. Anyway, back then it was post-hippie days when everybody was into peace and love and I just wanted to be a rock star or something. So I quit after four months and it was a bit of a catastrophe for my father because he expected me to go into his old regiment. The atmosphere at home got quite bad, and I just decided to run away really. I got this job in South America through an uncle of a friend of mine who knew somebody who had a ranch, and I stayed there for a year before I went to university.

MR: A lot of your books concern exactly that anxiety about what happens in war and what happens in some kind of conflict. Is part of the old army experience coming out there, do you suppose?

LdeB: The four months in the army were very helpful in a number of ways. I actually do know what it's like to dig a trench all night, or to fire a machine gun, or throw a hand grenade that you can only throw fifteen yards, but that can kill for fifty yards. And I know what it's like to be in the manure, together with a bunch of blokes who are your comrades.

MR: Are you conscious of anchoring everything very much in concrete experience?

LdeB: I can't really say. It *feels* as though everything comes straight out of my imagination, but I've no doubt that you can trace most things back to one thing or another. Not just my experiences though; I'm very dependent on other people's experiences. For example, I sat my father down and interviewed him about what it was like to go into battle, because at one point I needed that information and he had never talked about his war experience in any detail, for obvious reasons: I mean, it was too painful. But he did talk. For the account of the earthquake in *Captain Corelli*, I relied on a Greek who fortuitously turned up at the house next door. I interviewed him, because he'd been in it. So I do rely very much on other people's experience as well as my own, and I have to try and imagine what it was like to be there from what they tell me.

MR: While you have these huge casts of characters that come from all different walks of life, the other thing that comes across is this sense of a really big space. You cover a lot of actual territory, a lot of places, different places, and time –

huge spans of time – it's never small in that sense either. People grow old and have grandchildren within the space of your novels. How much do you need that really big space?

LdeB: Well, if I only need small spaces, it turns out to be a short story. A short story can only occupy half an hour of anyone's life – of a character's life, I mean. I just temperamentally seem to be more at home with a huge canvas than a small one. I really don't want to get bogged down with what kind of brocade people have on their curtains, and how many lumps of sugar they put in their tea, I can live without that kind of detail. And I also have this propensity for building novels up rather like jigsaw puzzles, with bits and pieces from all over the place. So I've got a politician ranting on in one place, and I've got people, say, peasants damming a stream in another scene, and the books come together as a huge collage. And often I don't sort out the order of the chapters until I've written all of them. I never start a book at the beginning either. Usually I just write the bits I fancy the most first, and then fill in the rest after. With a computer it's easy to do that, but actually that's the way I even did it with my first novel, when I was writing longhand.

MR: Is that part of why you often return? Start a story in one place, and then come back to it?

LdeB: That's exactly it. In *Don Emmanuel* I think I had three or four stories going on simultaneously to begin with, and I wrote them all individually, and then when it came to sorting the chapters out it was a question of 'one for you, one for you, one for you', so you were going back and forth between the narratives.

MR: Even when the narratives don't absolutely connect, the

reader comes upon a kind of irony because sometimes there's a contradiction in one story or another, or they rub up against one another. I'm particularly thinking of the chapter in *Captain Corelli* where Carlo goes and sees Francesco's mother, and you have the truth and what he's actually saying side by side. It's almost as though the chapters allow a reader to do that, to draw their own conclusions.

LdeB: Yes, and it's made much easier by the way that I use first-person narratives. A lot of my characters tell their own story, which means that they can have slightly different versions, or disagreements, with other parts of the narrative. We're all familiar with the idea of the unreliable narrator. I don't normally have the writer writing from an omniscient point of view. I have a few chapters like that, but not all that many, and most of the narrative is built up with other people's stories.

MR: Have you any idea what sort of personality your omniscient narrator is?

LdeB: Is that asking me who I am?

MR: In a way. Or who your writing persona is perhaps.

LdeB: I do have a sort of Louis de Bernières persona, but that's when I put on my linen jacket and go to literary festivals, and I can just play at being Louis de Bernières. Obviously, I'm not like that at home when I'm with the cat and I've got the hoovering to do. But from a literary point of view, I often have that feeling, which I think many other writers or musicians have, of being a conduit, a telephone line, and it's almost like voices are coming through you. It could be a kind of madness for all I know. It's like a schizophrenic hearing voices, but in my case the madness is sort of under control and I'm making good use of it. When the writing's going really well, that's how I feel. I feel like it's someone else writing through me, with a part of my mind that I'm perhaps not normally connected with in everyday life.

MR: And the story takes you over, and it is more than you?

LdeB: Yes it does, and it is, and the story more often than not doesn't go the way I planned it, so I have to alter the plot as I go along. The characters start to misbehave and do their own thing.

MR: Because you so often use a first-person narrative, it means you do have different points of view, and they're subjective. One of the things that indicates is that you really distrust history – or the official version.

LdeB: I do distrust history very much for a number of reasons. One is that new evidence, new testimony, new witnesses are always coming to light. The other is that most history is written by people who have an interest in their side coming well out of the story. So, for example, the French know of lots of battles they won against us, which we've never heard of. And of course we've won lots of battles against them that they have never heard of. This gets you worried. As time goes by we change ideologically. So, for example, at one time it was quite customary to read histories of empires, as if empires were great and wonderful things. Alexander the Great is called *the Great*, but he was actually a megalomaniac who cried when there was nothing left to conquer. So whereas in Greece today he's still greatly admired, and I suppose all over the world he is greatly admired, I think he was probably crazy. We are always revising history, you see, so it's difficult to write as if there's a final version. There's always more to come. Sometimes you have to take a risk. Much of my first novel was taken up with writing about what happened in the torture chambers of South America, in Argentina and Uruguay and Chile and places like that, and over that sort of issue, you have, in the end, to take sides. You may not like or approve of the people who were taken in and tortured – a great many of them were communists, for example, in Chile, and I don't have any time for communism – but it is such an atrocious thing to torture people, and to forbid them to think for themselves that I'm on the side of those people who were tortured. You have to make those decisions.

MR: In those three books, and especially in *Señor Vivo and the Coca Lord*, there are a lot of really horrible, physical descriptions of torture and other terrible things. How hard is it to write that?

LdeB: There was one scene in *Señor Vivo*, in Chapter 49, which was the hardest thing to write, and that's when Anica is cut up in the chrysanthemum house – it's a horrible scene, I often get letters of protest about it – and after I wrote it I felt so shaken that I had to stop writing for two weeks. But the point was that I felt I had a duty to tell the truth. In Colombia in particular, ever since the 1950s when there was a great period of political violence called *la violencia*, they had been specialising in developing new ways of slowly torturing people to death. The cocaine people took over these techniques and refined them and they are still used today. So I felt I had a duty to the truth. I want to point out to Westerners that every time they use cocaine, they do it on the dead body of an innocent Colombian. It's as simple as that.

MR: So you do feel very strongly that there is a moral responsibility?

LdeB: Yes.

MR: You just used the phrase about people who think for themselves. That's in the dedication to *The Troublesome Offspring of Cardinal Guzman*, isn't it?

LdeB: Yes. People thought that it was something to do with Salman Rushdie, but it wasn't. I was just thinking of everybody who'd died as a result of just having their own ideas, however barmy they are. In the case of *The Troublesome Offspring of Cardinal Guzman*, I took most of the events for that from what happened in the Middle Ages in the South of France, when the northern French invaded Provence, in order to eradicate the Cathar culture, loot its wealth, and impose their own ideas. It so happens that until quite recently in Latin America these sorts of crusades by fanatics were fairly common, so I just moved those events to my imaginary Latin-American country. At the siege of one city Simon de Montfort was asked, 'How do we know which are the heretics, so we can kill them?', and he replied, 'Kill them all. God will know his own.' I have my character saying that in the book.

MR: There's a long reverie in *Don Emmanuel* about the difference between patriotism and nationalism. Is this something that exercises you?

LdeB: Well, I feel patriotic about a lot of countries in the sense that I love them. I love my own country, I love France, I love Greece, I love Spain and so on. I think that nationalism is patriotism at somebody else's expense. You're exalting your own country above others, and that is what I think is really wicked. I really hate and despise that kind of nationalism, because it's so stupid. It is, after all, a mere accident of birth where you are born. Any of us could have been born in

Somaliland, for God's sake. That wouldn't make us any better or worse. I feel very, very uncomfortable in the presence of nationalism. One of the things that makes me feel uncomfortable about Greeks and Turks is that, for example, they are very nationalist. I think it's on a level with religion. Religion and nationalism, as Bertrand Russell says, they're the things that cause wars and prevent marriages.

MR: The other thing that Latin America gives you as a venue is that sense of there being a genuine spirituality as well as all the horrible things. There are lots of beautiful images and places and ideas. Does the element of magic – if that's the right word – appeal to you?

LdeB: I am very interested in magic, and have been interested in various religions at different times. I think that what's nice about magic is that behind it lies the idea that reality may be other than we suppose, and you might be able to make a difference in our everyday reality by using this other reality which is hidden behind appearances. It's a lovely idea, but I don't really know if there's any truth in it. My own spirituality is more instinctive than articulated. I get my religion from watching the sun go down over the sea. I don't get it by going into cathedrals or going to services.

MR: There's also the magic of fiction, the fact that you can imagine a place that actually doesn't exist . . .

LdeB: There is something magical about fiction, and about poetry, and the ability to compose music, and even more magical, I think, is the ability to *play* music. If you were looking at it from a Darwinian point of view, you can't really see the point. What's the point of being able to make up stories about people who don't exist? It seems a very strange thing to do, and it may even be uniquely human. Perhaps it's part of the universal human madness, but I can't really explain why we love it so much, and why we need it so much. Except that, in one way, it does help to explain us to ourselves. You know, there's a syndrome which a lot of readers get into, which is thinking that their life is like a novel. I've fallen into this myself when I was younger, sort of wondering why the real world wasn't quite working out. Writing exposes you to the truth about all sorts of things. So that, for example, when I first started writing, I was under this delusion that I was some kind of a pacifist. But as soon as I started writing and was talking about these horrendous things going on in my imaginary Latin-American country, I very quickly realised that you actually have an obligation to resist oppression. It's a moral duty. And so I lost my pacifism almost straight away. I also discovered that I was actually very interested in violence and its effects, which is something I never would have expected in myself, I thought I was much nicer than that. And I've only just now lost this interest in violence, and I don't put it in my books much any more.

MR: That said, I was struck by the way that you come back to the problem of the way that people get brutalised by particular circumstances. I mean, the most obvious, and, in a way the case that you explore most fully, is that of Mandras in *Captain Corelli*, but it's there in Federico, in *Don Emmanuel*, and in so many of the characters. The whole treatment of that subject is very generous and thoughtful. It obviously is something that has intrigued you.

LdeB: Yes. In the case of Mandras, he was corrupted – and I still think of him as being a complete innocent – by an absolutist ideology that seemed to have an answer to everything you could have ever asked. Which was, I suppose, the Stalinist version of Marxism which was current at his time, when every-body on the left still thought Stalin was wonderful. In my third novel I'm worried about the effects of religious ideology – again, absolutist and authoritarian. It permits people *not* to think for themselves. To follow an absolutist ideology gives them some sort of moral pretext for doing things that they would never otherwise have done. So you can kill someone in the name of your country, you can kill someone in the name of your faith or your political ideal. Even if you are the kind of person who, walking down a street, would never dream of killing anybody. You're given permission to be bad.

VINTAGE
LIVING
TEXTS

Captain Corelli's Mandolin

IN CLOSE-UP

Reading guides

CAPTAIN CORELLI'S MANDOLIN

BEFORE YOU BEGIN TO READ . . .
THE TITLE
Why do you think that de Bernières has given this title to his novel? Note that we don't meet Captain Corelli until page 188. Work through the novel and analyse the significances of the mandolin. Remember also that the mandolin has a name.

THEMES
If you look at the interview with de Bernières, you will see that he discusses the themes of

- War and its effects
- Love and forgiveness
- The idea of Greece
- Fiction and reality
- The value of myths and stories
- Attitudes to history

While you are reading *Captain Corelli's Mandolin* and the Latin-American trilogy in detail it is worth bearing these overall themes in mind. At the end of this detailed reading guide you will find suggested contexts, which will help you to situate the themes in relation to the novel as a whole. The reading activities given below are not designed to be followed slavishly. Choose whichever sections most interest you or are most useful for your own purposes. The questions that are set at the end of the chapter plan are to help you relate each individual chapter to the novel as a whole.

Reading activities: detailed analysis

CAPTAIN CORELLI'S MANDOLIN

DEDICATION

Read de Bernières's dedication of the novel to his mother and
father. *Captain Corelli's Mandolin* is one of a number of contemporary novels in which the writers attempt to understand
the wartime world of their parents' generation. Comparisons
can be made in this respect with Ian McEwan's *Atonement* or
Sebastian Faulks's *Charlotte Gray*.

PREFATORY POEM: 'THE SOLDIER'

What does this poem say about young deaths in war? The subject has been widely treated in poetry, especially poetry of the
First World War. Compare Wolfe's poem with Brooke's sonnet
of the same title. Published in 1914, at the very start of World
War One, Brooke's poem seems idealistic, even meaningless,
to a reader who knows what came afterwards. In what ways
could Wolfe's poem be seen as a knowing comment on
Brooke's? As you read *Captain Corelli's Mandolin*, consider what
the novel is saying about the death of young soldiers in war.

CHAPTER I
(pp. 1–9)

Focus on: characterisation

ANALYSE . . .

How does the episode in which Dr Iannis treats Stamatis present the characters of the doctor, Stamatis and his wife? Pelagia figures only briefly in this chapter, but later she will become a central character. What are your first impressions of her?

Focus on: sense of place

RESEARCH . . .

Choose three of the characters from Greek myth cited by Dr Iannis. Using a dictionary of Classical Mythology, look up these characters and read the various stories ascribed to them. What do these references suggest about how the Cephallonians' awareness of their history moulds how that they see themselves?

Focus on: language

TRANSFORM . . .

Taking pages 1–3, underline all of the unusual and extravagant words that are used and make a list of them. If you are unfamiliar with them, look them up. Find a commonplace equivalent for each and write it down. Try re-reading these pages with these ordinary words in place of their originals. Discuss the effects that changing these words has.

Looking over Chapter 1

QUESTIONS FOR ESSAYS OR DISCUSSION

1.   'I feel that the English language is so rich, that you ought to exploit it' (de Bernières). In what ways has de Bernières exploited language in this opening chapter?

2.   How do the language and classical allusions in this chapter present Dr Iannis's character and way of thinking? In your answer you should

- look closely at the use of language and narrative method
- comment on the place of issues such as Dr Iannis's level of education and the importance of the past as part of the island's identity

CHAPTER 2
(pp. 10–18)

Focus on: Fascism

RESEARCH THE CONTEXT . . .

Look up 'Fascism' in a dictionary of ideas (such as *The New Fontana Dictionary of Modern Thought*), or in an encyclopaedia. Write a list of the five main ideas that informed most Fascist movements. Read the extract from the entry on Fascism that Mussolini wrote for the Italian Encyclopaedia in 1932, reproduced in the Contexts section. Look up 'megalomania' in a dictionary, or better, in a dictionary of psychology. Compare these ideas with the Duce's thoughts in this chapter.

TRANSFORM . . .

Turn the Duce's beliefs into a series of political slogans. Are they easily encapsulated in this way? What is the use of political slogans?

READ CLOSELY . . .

To gain an insight in Mussolini's methods, read the excerpts from his speech to the Blackshirts, delivered in Rome on February 23rd, 1941, which are reproduced in Contexts section. How does he use the image of authority to manipulate his audience?

Focus on: images

EXAMINE . . .

Examine the Duce's emphasis on the importance of images, and on presenting himself as the epitome of virility.

Focus on: narrative technique

COMPARE . . .

De Bernières's narrative technique in this chapter has some qualities in common with the 'dramatic monologue', a poetic form in which a character is depicted by his way of speaking, and usually betrays himself by saying more than he meant to. Read Browning's poem 'My Last Duchess', and compare the way the poet has employed the form of the dramatic monologue to portray the speaker with de Bernières's use of narrative technique in this chapter.

Focus on: the background

TRANSFORM . . .

Pick one character apart from the Duce, and re-write his or her presentation in the chapter from that character's point of view. Convey your chosen character's attitudes to the Duce, and why your character behaves as he or she does in the Duce's presence. Now consider the effect of the absence of these other voices in the original.

Looking over Chapter 2

QUESTIONS FOR ESSAYS OR DISCUSSION

1. How does de Bernières control our reactions to the Duce in this chapter? In particular, how does de Bernières employ irony to betray the limitations and self-delusions of the Duce's mind?

2. 'The portrait never quits the easy level of unpleasant comedy' (Francis Spufford). How valid is this criticism of de Bernières's satirical portrait of Il Duce, in your opinion?

CHAPTER 3
(pp. 19–25)

Focus on: character

COMPARE . . .
— The juxtaposition of this chapter with the last, and Velisarios's first name, 'Megalo', invite us to compare the village strongman with the political strongman, the megalomaniac Duce. Compare and contrast the two characters.

Focus on: narrative voice and point of view

CONSIDER THE NARRATIVE VOICE . . .
— After the delusional narrative viewpoint of the Duce in Chapter 2, the narrative now switches to another voice. Analyse

the ways in which the narrator in this chapter seems to carry 'authority', as if it represents something close to the author's own point of view. Is the authorial 'voice' ever intrusive? (If you are unfamiliar with this idea, look up the term 'intrusive narrator' in the glossary of literary terms.)

TRANSFORM . . .
— Rewrite the events of this chapter in the form of a monologue by Velisarios. Consider the effects of changing the narrative point of view in this way.

Looking over Chapter 3

QUESTIONS FOR ESSAYS OR DISCUSSION
The use and the abuse of strength and violence will become central themes in this novel. Comment on the way Velisarios employs his strength in this chapter. In your answer you should

- look closely at the use of language and narrative technique
- comment on the place of relevant issues such as the attitudes of the villagers and the conventions of Cephallonian village life, as they are evident in the novel so far
- think about what we learn about Pelagia in this chapter.

CHAPTER 4
(pp. 26–9)

Focus on: the narrative frame

COMPARE . . .
— In this chapter the narrative is framed as a secret 'testament' by Guercio about his nature and about his most personal

feelings. How does a testament suit his character and experiences better than a monologue?

Focus on: the theme of homosexuality

RESEARCH AND DISCUSS . . .

— Guercio's narrative presents the prevalent attitudes to homosexuality in Italy at the time. Summarise these attitudes as he presents them. He also alludes to attitudes to homosexuality in ancient Greece. Discuss where you might research these further, and then do so, making a list of the main ideas. Do the same for attitudes towards homosexuality expressed in the Old Testament of the Bible. If you want to gain a fuller idea of attitudes to homosexuality in the early twentieth century in Europe, read E. M. Forster's *Maurice* (completed 1914).

Focus on: the language of love

CREATE A MAP . . .

— Look for the words and phrases that Guercio uses to describe and express his feelings of love and the ideals that he attaches to love in this chapter. Create a 'map' which connects all of the words that you have identified, grouping them into semantic fields. Keep adding to this diagram as you read the later chapters narrated by Guercio.

Looking over Chapter 4

QUESTIONS FOR ESSAYS OR DISCUSSION

1. How does Guercio conceive of love?

2. Given what you have seen of Mussolini's ideology so far, what might be the significance of the fact that de Bernières has chosen to represent a member of the Italian militia as a homosexual individualist who feels love passionately?

CHAPTER 5
(pp. 30–6)

Focus on: characterisation and language

COMPARE CHARACTERS AND ATTITUDES . . .
— As you read pp. 30–3 (up to 'the vacuum left by the Turks'), underline the words and phrases which indicate Metaxas's value system. List what he admires and what he despises in two columns. Then compare the portrayal of Metaxas in this chapter with the portrayal of the Duce in Chapter 2. What contrasts and what parallels can you find? What do you infer about the similarities and differences between the two characters from a comparison of the language that they use?

Focus on: narrative technique

LIST AND COMMENT . . .
— This chapter adds another narrative strategy to those already used in the novel. The narrator presents Metaxas in the third person (i.e. the narrator's point of view is distinct from Metaxas's), but the narrative style closely reflects the character's 'voice' and ways of thinking. List all of the narrative techniques used so far in the novel, and give a brief summary of the effects each creates.

Looking over Chapter 5

QUESTIONS FOR ESSAYS OR DISCUSSION
1. Comment on the way that this chapter presents Metaxas. In your answer you should

● look closely at the use of language and narrative technique
● comment on the place of relevant issues such as his status

as Prime Minister and the political situation in Europe at
the time

Remember that the title of the chapter is explained in
Chapter 14.

2. Through a consideration of this chapter and also of
Chapter 2 ('The Duce'), discuss the validity of the claim that
fiction is not a suitable vehicle for presenting real figures from
history because it is made up. Then consider the claim that 'history' is just fiction that attempts to represent the facts as we
know them.

CHAPTER 6
(pp. 37–43)

Focus on: the narrative strategy

FIND LINKS . . .
— The four separate narratives that the novel has presented
so far (events in a village in Cephallonia, the Duce's thoughts,
Metaxas's worries and Guercio's testament) now begin to come
together, and will be interwoven more and more closely as the
novel progresses. Look for the small details that link Guercio's
narrative in this chapter with the three other narrative threads.
Whenever you come across an allusion to a detail that has
already been mentioned, create a cross-reference by writing the
page numbers of the other reference in the margin next to each
instance (a useful shorthand to indicate a cross-reference is to
write, for example, 'cf. p. 10' in the margin). You will find, for
instance, that the Duce's monologue in Chapter 2 alludes to
numerous details that are picked up again later, when we see
the catastrophic effects of his extreme ideas on ordinary people.

Focus on: the theme of guilt

COMMENT . . .

— Guercio's testament is an act of propitiation, not for his 'forbidden' love of another man, but for 'abominable and filthy deeds' carried out in war. These two adjectives were often applied to homosexual sex by those who disapproved. What point is Guercio making about levels of guilt? How does this idea affect the way you see the Duce, who wages war for reasons that are morally bankrupt, yet idealises 'virility' (p. 11)?

Focus on: love

— If you started the map exercise on Chapter 4, continue to develop it as you read this chapter.

TRANSFORM . . .

— Write a poem as if by Guercio about Francesco. Select and use some of the language that Guercio uses on pp. 40–1 when he describes Francesco. Take care to mix 'masculine' and 'feminine' words and images, as Guercio does in that passage. Write a commentary on your poem, explaining why you have chosen the language you have to express Guercio's feelings.

Looking over Chapter 6

QUESTIONS FOR ESSAYS OR DISCUSSION

1. Refer back to the Duce's comments about Italian soldiers on page 11. Discuss the ways in which his comments about the ideal military man are challenged by the presentation of Guercio in this chapter.

2. 'The ultimate truth is that history ought to consist only of the anecdotes of the little people who are caught up in it' (p. 40). Dr Iannis decides when writing his History that

'objectivity was quite unattainable' (p. 4). How does de Bernières's version of history confront these issues, both in this chapter and throughout the novel?

CHAPTER 7
(pp. 44–52)

Focus on: caricature

COMPARE . . .
— The stock characters and undignified situations of this chapter give the comedy and tragedy that afflict them a quality of parody. Can you think of other instances in literature of the types that figure here: the drunken cleric, the doting and humiliated young lover, the henpecked husband? How does de Bernières render their potentially tragic situations (Father Arsenios is a miserable failure; Mandras's love is doomed; Stamatis loathes his wife) as essentially comic?

Focus on: narrative tone

TRANSFORM . . .
— Look at Dr Iannis's conversation with Stamatis, from 'It's my wife, you see' on p. 51 to 'O God' on p. 52. Keeping the dialogue exactly the same, rewrite the narrative between their lines of speech in order to create a serious tone. See how economically this radically different effect can be created, and discuss what you find. What does this reveal about how de Bernières creates a comic effect in the original?

Looking over Chapter 7

QUESTIONS FOR ESSAYS OR DISCUSSION
1. Dr Iannis emerges as a sceptic – about religion, about noble

causes, about humanity's ability to learn. His sense of humour can be malicious. But he is also a principled and humane man. Analyse how de Bernières conveys these aspects of his character in this chapter.

2. How does de Bernières create comic effects in the construction of the characters and the scenes in this chapter? In your answer you should

● identify the words and phrases that carry the greatest comic effect
● comment on the place of relevant issues such as the attitudes to the Church, to love and to marriage in the Cephallonia region at the time.

CHAPTER 8
(pp. 53–9)

Focus on: Communism

RESEARCH . . .
— Look up 'Communism' in a dictionary of ideas, or in an encyclopaedia. What is the origin of the word 'Communism'? Write a list of the five main ideas that inform Communist thought, and compare them with your list of Fascist ideas from Chapter 2. Do these opposite extremes of political ideology have anything in common?

Focus on: characterisation

MAKE COMPARISONS . . .
— Compare Dr Iannis's reaction to the 'funny cat' on p. 55 with the Duce's act of shooting the cat on p. 18. What do their contrasting reactions reveal about the two characters?

Focus on: father and daughter

TRANSFORM . . .

— Pelagia 'entered, convinced that her father had seen her kissing Mandras. She was preparing an obdurate defence' (p. 58). Based on your impressions so far of Pelagia's character, intelligence and language, write the defence that she might have made, had her father exploded. Discuss why you have given her the arguments and the language that you have.

Looking over Chapter 8

QUESTIONS FOR ESSAYS OR DISCUSSION

1. Dr Iannis comments that 'Children see more than we do' (p. 56). Consider how the incident with Lemoni in this chapter illustrates this idea.

2. Compare what Dr Iannis *wants* to do in this chapter with what he *actually* does. What does he reveal about his nature by what he does?

CHAPTER 9
(pp. 60–7)

Focus on: context

DISCUSS . . .

— Why might it be significant that the chapter title is the first mention of a specific date in the novel?

RESEARCH . . .

— In the Contexts section of this book you will find an extract of an open letter from Vlakhos to Hitler which refers to the

Italian sinking of the *Elli* at Tinos. Read it. What significance did the Greeks attach to this incident?

Focus on: father and daughter's suitor

TRANSFORM . . .
— Dr Iannis tells Mandras to 'stop being so polite' (p. 65). Rewrite their conversation, this time portraying Mandras as an arrogant thug. See how few changes you need to make to create the desired effect, then consider the touches that de Bernières has used to create the effect of Mandras's excessive desire to please.

Looking over Chapter 9

QUESTIONS FOR ESSAYS OR DISCUSSION
1. 'We should care for each other more than we care for ideas,' says Dr Iannis (p. 62). How has de Bernières established this idea as a key theme in the novel so far?

2. Analyse the ways in which this chapter presents the villagers as humorous, warm and humane. In your answer you should

● look closely at the use of language and dialogue
● comment on the place of issues such as the villagers' tight-knit community, their sense of the past and the Italian attack at Tinos.

CHAPTER 10
(pp. 68–74)

Focus on: the theme of guilt

— Guercio's account clearly seeks to vindicate his actions.

Sometimes a novelist will call into question a narrator's relia-
bility if his intentions are self-serving. How does the narrative
here support Guercio's account, and suggest that he is to be
trusted to tell the truth?

Focus on: satire and language

EXAMINE AND DISCUSS . . .
— Read the account of Guercio and Francesco's meeting with
Rivolta on pp. 69–71. Identify the words and phrases about the
colonel that carry the most satirical effect. Discuss their connotations. See if you can change any of them for words with
similar meanings but ones which have no satirical effect. How
dependent is the satirical effect on the characteristics that Rivolta
is given, and how dependent is it on the effects of the language
used to describe these?

TRANSFORM . . .
— Read the account of the men's anticipation of the
approaching combat on pp. 71–3 ('I do not think . . .' to '. . .
lose each other to a bullet'). Select the words that most effectively convey their attitude towards the operation they have
been told to carry out. Consider the connotations of these
words. Write the text of an advertisement for an army recruit-
ment campaign using some of these words.

Looking over Chapter 10

QUESTIONS FOR ESSAYS OR DISCUSSION
1. 'Moral outrage is boring and predictable. Satire is far more
effective' (de Bernières). How effective do you find the use of
satire to convey moral anger in Chapter 10?

2. With reference to this chapter and to Chapter 2, discuss
the theme of honour in the novel so far.

CHAPTER 11
(pp. 75–83)

Focus on: voice and point of view in section 1
(pp. 75–6)

ANALYSE . . .
— Write down the individual topics of each of Pelagia's thoughts. Consider how one flows into another, work out the metaphoric connections between them. Is this description or dramatised account of Pelagia's thought processes effective? Are you convinced by the tone of her voice?

RESEARCH AND COMPARE . . .
— Read Virginia Woolf's essay 'Modern Fiction' (1919). Here Woolf proposes that the experimental novelist must endeavour to reproduce some imitation of 'life', that is, the myriad shifting thoughts and impressions of consciousness as they appear haphazardly (or not) throughout each day. In what way might you view de Bernières's technique as one that can usefully be compared to the terms of Woolf's manifesto? In what ways might de Bernières's method differ entirely from that recommended by Woolf?

Focus on: rhetoric and tone of voice in section 2
(pp. 76–7)

EXAMINE . . .
— This first passage where Mandras speaks in his own first-person voice is couched in the form of a prayer. How do you know that? Which references and speaking or narrative patterns make that prayer evident? What does the use of this particular narrative form suggest about the character of Mandras? How do these references help to give shape to the character of Mandras?

Focus on: allusions to myth in section 4
(pp. 79–81)

COMPARE . . .
— Read this classical legend about the fate of Arion:

Next to him in musical fame was Arion, the musician who won untold wealth by his talent. On one occasion, having gone to Sicily to take part in a musical contest which had attracted thither the most famous musicians from all points of the compass, he resolved to return home by sea.

Unfortunately for him, the vessel upon which he had embarked was manned by an avaricious, piratical crew who, having heard of his treasures, resolved to murder him to obtain possession of them. He was allowed but scant time to prepare for death; but, just as they were about to toss him overboard, he craved permission to play for the last time. The pirates consented. His clear notes floated over the sea, and allured a school of dolphins, which came and played about the ship. The pirates, terrified by the power of his music, and in dread lest their hearts should be moved, quickly laid hands upon him, and hurled him into the water, where he fell upon the broad back of a dolphin, who bore him in safety to the nearest shore.

There was there heard a most celestiall sound
Of dainty musicke, which did next ensew
Before the spouse: that was Arion crownd;
Who, playing on his harpe, unto him drew
The eares and hearts of all that goodly crew,
That even yet the Dolphin, which him bore

Through the Agean seas from Pirates vew,
Stood still by him astonisht at his lore,
And all the raging seas for joy forgot to rore.

– Edmund Spenser

To commemorate this miracle, the gods placed
Arion's harp, together with the dolphin, in the
heavens, where they form a constellation.

*The Myths of Greece and Rome: Their Stories, Signification
and Origin* H. A. Guerber (George Harrap &
Company, London, 1907), pp. 63–4.

In what ways might the story of Arion connect to the story
of Mandras? Why is it important that this section begins with
a song, and ends with Mandras's swim with the dolphins?
— How does the characterisation of Mandras played out here
in this passage affect your attitude to him and his actions
throughout the rest of the novel?

Focus on: the theme of men and women in section 5
(pp. 81–2)

DESCRIBE AND ASSESS . . .
— Pelagia thinks about her dead mother Mitera. Note down
the ways in which Mitera is described. What is Mandras's attitude to his mother? What is Pelagia's? How do their views
differ?

Focus on: narrative viewpoint in section 7
(p. 83)

CONSIDER . . .
— Why is it Pelagia that ends this two-voiced sequence?

Looking over Chapter 11

QUESTIONS FOR ESSAYS OR DISCUSSION

1. Why might de Bernières have chosen to present the two different viewpoints of these characters in direct, first-person speech? What effect does it have on your attitude to these characters – and to the way they relate to each other – to be allowed to see the private hopes and fears of each?

2. 'It's not so much the story of a woman, as the story of an island and a race and a lost time.' In what ways do the methods and themes of this chapter relate to the methods and themes of the novel as a whole?

CHAPTER 12
(pp. 84–97)

Focus on: religion

DISCUSS . . .
— What does the cult of St Gerasimos seem to signify for the Cephallonians?
— Examine how pagan and Christian practices co-exist in the carnival. Do the pagan elements enrich their faith or debase it?

Looking over Chapter 12

QUESTIONS FOR ESSAYS OR DISCUSSION

1. What role does the Church seem to play in Cephallonian life?

2. Choose three paragraphs from this chapter and discuss them as examples of de Bernières's imagination for detail. In your answer you should

- look closely at language and narrative method
- comment on the place of issues such as the social attitudes and habits that govern the characters you are discussing.

3. In Chapter 5 Metaxas referred to 'the wild, irresponsible individualism of the Greeks' (p. 33). Discuss how the Greeks are depicted in this description of the carnival.

CHAPTER 13
(pp. 98–107)

Focus on: Pelagia's inner conflict

EXAMINE . . .
— Pelagia is intoxicated by Mandras's beauty, but anxiously aware that they are not well matched. Examine how de Bernières conveys her conflicted feelings for him in this chapter.

COMPARE AND CONTRAST . . .
— Read Virginia Woolf's essay 'Professions for Women' (1931). In this essay, Woolf argues that it is essential for any writer, but especially for a woman writer working in the shadow of the nineteenth century, not to be constricted by conventions that demand that a woman's thoughts are 'pure'. How might you relate this chapter to the arguments in Woolf's essay?

Looking over Chapter 13

QUESTIONS FOR ESSAYS OR DISCUSSION
1. De Bernières has been criticised for sentimentalising poverty. With reference to Chapter 13, and to previous chapters if you wish, discuss whether you think that this is a fair criticism.

2. In what ways is Pelagia caught between her own wishes and the role that women in Cephallonia at the time were expected to fulfil?

CHAPTER 14
(pp. 108–15)

Focus on: narrative voice

ANALYSE . . .
— What kind of 'voice' emerges in this chapter? Underline the key words that indicate the values that Grazzi lives by. What does he dislike most?

Focus on: Metaxas

COMPARE . . .
— 'Metaxas had earned his place in history amongst liberators, caesars and kings' (p. 115). Consider the historical significance of Metaxas's reaction. Metaxas's refusal brought Greece into the war as Britain's ally. Greece refused Mussolini's forces free passage, and drove them back through Albania. Had Greece agreed to surrender without resistance, Hitler might have invaded Russia in the spring, instead of making his disastrous attempt to take it in the winter. One could argue that Metaxas is owed a debt by Western nations for helping to preserve democracy against its enemies.
— 'There could not have been a man more different from the Duce' (p. 113). Compare your impressions of Metaxas here with your impressions of the Duce.

Looking over Chapter 14

QUESTIONS FOR ESSAYS OR DISCUSSION

1. Discuss the theme of honour in this chapter, and relate it to the treatment of this theme in the novel so far.

2. What impression do you form in this chapter of the Duce's methods?

CHAPTER 15
(pp. 116–24)

Focus on: language

TRANSFORM . . .

— Read the final four paragraphs, from 'We had become anonymous' to the end. How does Guercio emphasise the indignity of soldiers' suffering? Rewrite the passage, making only as many changes as are necessary to make it support the proposition that 'war is a wonderful thing'. What have you changed, and why?

Looking over Chapter 15

QUESTIONS FOR ESSAYS OR DISCUSSION

1. Discuss the theme of camaraderie in this chapter.

2. Analyse the way that Guercio portrays his experiences in this chapter. In your answer you should

- look closely at the language and imagery he uses
- comment on the place of relevant issues such as the nature of the Italian military campaign and hierarchy

CHAPTER 16
(pp. 125–33)

Focus on: the feminine perspective

COMPARE AND CONTRAST . . .

— 'I am no good at womanly things because my mother died when I was too young, and now I am having to try to learn all the things that I should have grown up with' (p. 129), writes Pelagia. Her letters are full of an awareness of the differences between the men's and women's roles. Read Alice Walker's influential essay 'In Search of Our Mother's Gardens' (1974), which is both about the specific creativity of her own mother, and about the ways in which women at different historical times, under different historical and cultural circumstances, have succeeded in making a space for their creative talents.

— Compare the ways in which Alice Walker's mother's garden might have some bearing on Pelagia's attempts at 'womanly things'. Where else in the novel as a whole are images of female creativity made the centre of the narrative?

Focus on: letters

CONSIDER . . .

— Letters are a one-sided conversation. Writers pen letters partly to communicate, but also to express themselves – to give their thoughts and feelings a shape. In what ways does Pelagia seem to be 'giving shape' to her confused feelings about Mandras in these letters? Do the letters betray changes in her feelings towards him?

Focus on: language

ANALYSE . . .

— Read the paragraph on pp. 127–8 ('All the news . . .'). What

do you infer about Pelagia's attitude to war from this paragraph? Underline the descriptive words and phrases. List the
abstract nouns. What are the connotations of these words?

Looking over Chapter 16

QUESTIONS FOR ESSAYS OR DISCUSSION

1.   What understanding of love does Pelagia have at this stage
in the novel?

2.   This chapter imitates the part of *The Odyssey* in which
Penelope, faithfully waiting for Odysseus to return from his
long travels, weaves a cloth and says she'll only marry one of
her many suitors when it's finished. Every night she unpicks
it. In Chapter 13, Pelagia had wondered, as she spied on
Mandras, whether 'in the time of Odysseus there had been
young girls like herself who had gone to the sea in order to
spy on the nakedness of those they loved. She shivered at the
thought of such a melting into history' (p. 106). By linking
Pelagia and Mandras with figures from myth and antiquity, what
is de Bernières saying about change and time?

CHAPTER 17
(pp. 134–40)

Focus on: language

ANALYSE . . .
— How effectively does de Bernières describe physical pain?
Pick out ten phrases that you find especially effective, and
analyse their effects.

Looking over Chapter 17

QUESTIONS FOR ESSAYS OR DISCUSSION
1.   'De Bernières' great skill is in portraying the resilience of individuals confronted by inhuman forces.' Discuss, with reference to any part of the novel so far.

2.   What evidence can you find in this or earlier chapters to support Guercio's claim that the war was 'frivolous' (p. 138)?

CHAPTER 18
(pp. 141–7)

Focus on: Dr Iannis's History

EVALUATE AND EXPLAIN . . .
— Dr Iannis has been struggling to find the right register for a History. Underline words and phrases in the excerpts in Chapter 18 that seem to you to hit the wrong register for this genre, and explain why they do so.

Focus on: identity

ASSESS TO WHAT EXTENT . . .
— Dr Iannis muses on the various roles he plays: as father, doctor, fount of wisdom, community leader, historian. To what extent are these roles defined by the community he lives in? How influential are social conventions on the lives of the Cephallonian characters?

Looking over Chapter 18

QUESTIONS FOR ESSAYS OR DISCUSSION
1.   De Bernières has described the relationship between Dr

55

Iannis and Pelagia as 'the key relationship. It's very sweet. They have a lot of respect for each other.' Discuss what this chapter shows of the love Dr Iannis has for his daughter.

2. What do the excerpts from Dr Iannis's writings add to the theme of the influence that history has on the present?

CHAPTER 19
(pp. 148–52)

Focus on: word choice

LIST AND CONTRAST . . .
— First, reread the story that Guercio tells Francesco's wife and mother, and underline the words that are intended to console them. List these words in their semantic groups. Then do the same for the passages that describe the truth. Compare the kinds of words that are used in each of the two accounts.

Focus on: what can and cannot be said

DISCUSS . . .
— Guercio finally expresses his love as Francesco dies. Consider the restraint that Guercio has shown. In the novel's moral scheme, how are Guercio's passion and noble restraint valued?
— Guercio cannot tell the women the truth because it is too brutal. Are there any kinds of truth that novels cannot say for the same reason – or for any other – or are novels privileged and capable of saying anything?

Focus on: missing perspectives

ROLE PLAY AND ARTICULATE . . .
— In a group of four: one of you reads Guercio's account of Francesco's death, section by section. A second reads the account of what really happened. A third articulates what Francesco's mother thinks in response to each section of Guercio's account. A fourth does the same for Francesco's wife. At the end, discuss the significance of the absence of the women's perspectives in the novel.

Looking over Chapter 19

QUESTIONS FOR ESSAYS OR DISCUSSION
1.   Discuss the friendship between Francesco and Guercio in this chapter and earlier, and relate it to the theme of love in the novel as a whole.

2.   Comment on the effects created by the mixture of senti-mentality and brutality in this chapter.

CHAPTER 20
(pp. 153–8)

Focus on: imagery

COMPARE . . .
— 'It seemed inconceivable that this desolate ghost concealed the soul and body of the man she had loved and desired and missed so much' (p. 156). Read the description of Mandras on pp. 154–5 ('The stranger wore . . . no trace of cuticles'), and compare this description with that on pp. 105–6 ('As though answering . . . sweep out to sea'). Make a list of the main images used in each description, and compare them.

Focus on: names

RESEARCH AND DISCUSS . . .
— Look up 'mandrake' in a dictionary such as *Brewer's Dictionary of Phrase and Fable*. Are there any associations that might link the mandrake to Mandras? Now consider the possible significance of the names of some of the other invented characters in the text: Pelagia, Corelli, Weber, Hector.

Looking over Chapter 20

QUESTIONS FOR ESSAYS OR DISCUSSION
1. How do you react to Mandras in this chapter? Reflect upon your feelings, and discuss how de Bernières manipulates your responses.

2. Mandras and Guercio fought on opposite sides. What does it say about the novel's moral scheme, that the sufferings of ordinary people on both sides are recounted in detail?

CHAPTER 21
(pp. 159–67)

Focus on: Pelagia

COMPARE AND COMMENT . . .
— Read pp. 161–6 and compare the comments that Drosoula makes about her son's appearance with Pelagia's assessment. De Bernières has said of Pelagia that 'she's very unusual for a Greek girl of that time in that she's been highly educated by her father'. Comment on your impressions of Pelagia in this chapter.

DISCUSS . . .
- 'You fall in love with the person, not the body.'
- 'Love enters by the eyes and also leaves by the eyes.'

— Which statement do you agree with more?

Looking over Chapter 21

QUESTION FOR ESSAYS OR DISCUSSION
1. Discuss the ways that the two women react to each other in this chapter.

CHAPTER 22
(pp. 168–74)

Focus on: myth

COMPARE . . .
This chapter forms a parallel with Odysseus's experiences on his epic journey home in *The Odyssey*. Odysseus arrived at the Island of Aeaea, home of the enchantress Circe, a powerful witch who turned his men to swine. Odysseus alone was immune to her magic. He was said to have stayed as her lover, before receiving her aid for the last part of his journey.
— Read Book X of *The Odyssey* in translation and compare the two accounts. What point is de Bernières making by this allusion to Homer?

DISCUSS . . .
It is a commonplace of twentieth-century Western literature that the world wars of the last century, combined with discoveries in science and psychology, undermined, in the eyes of many, the authority of religion. This idea is reflected in

Mandras's comment that the way he was tricked out of his virginity 'was all just one small part of the way in which God had turned His face away and consigned us all to the malice and caprices of the dark' (p. 173). Twentieth-century literature has sometimes sought to rework old myths as a way of making sense out of a world that is apparently godless.

— Discuss the ways in which *Captain Corelli's Mandolin* attempts to affirm meaning and value in the face of the evils it represents.

RE-CREATE . . .

— Based on your reading of this chapter (as well as of Book X of *The Odyssey*, or of other mythical stories), create a myth of your own about the power of love or about fate. Use symbols and a language that are appropriate to the genre. Then write a commentary on your own myth, explaining its moral scheme.

Looking over Chapter 22

QUESTIONS FOR ESSAYS OR DISCUSSION

1. What use does de Bernières make of mythical images and symbols in this chapter?

2. 'I had realised that we humans are blameless.' Discuss the theme of guilt in the novel so far.

CHAPTER 23
(pp. 175–89)

Focus on: context

READ AND COMPARE . . .

— In the Contexts section of this book you will find extracts from the text of the open letter from Vlakhos to Hitler that is alluded to on p. 177. Read these extracts and compare them with de Bernières's fictionalised account of the same events. What does the comparison tell you about de Bernières's use of historical events?

Focus on: the 'enemy'

COMPARE . . .

— Read what the villagers imagine about the 'enemy' early in this chapter and compare this with their first actual encounters with the Italian occupying force. How does de Bernières confound the villagers' (and the reader's) expectations? How does this initial impression confuse them? How does the final sentence emphasise the evident humanity of the 'enemy'?

Focus on: Corelli

WEIGH UP . . .

When Captain Corelli is first mentioned in the novel (already more than a third of the way through) the mandolin after which the novel is named enters with him (p. 188). De Bernières has said: 'If you ask the Greeks what they remember about the Italians, they say things like, "They were friendly . . . they tried to charm the girls (that was their main occupation), they played football and they played the mandolin." The Italians themselves are a bit fed up because this is a stereotype, but some stereotypes are true.'

— As you read on, weigh up to what extent Corelli is a national stereotype, the personification of Italy, and to what extent he is presented as a rounded individual.

Looking over Chapter 23

QUESTIONS FOR ESSAYS OR DISCUSSION

1.   Examine the way the villagers react to imminent invasion, and reflect on how their sense of history affects how they behave.

2.   'She surmised that this was what it must be like to be violated by a stranger' (p. 186). Assess Mandras's motives with regard to Pelagia in this chapter.

CHAPTER 24
(pp. 190–6)

Focus on: character and comic vignettes

INFER . . .

— What impression of Corelli's character do you get from the 'La Scala' vignette?

— Does the vignette of the Cephallonians' 'ungracious surrender' ring true to the way they have been presented in the novel so far? Look back to the Duce's plans of 'judicious intimidation that will weaken the Greek will' (p. 17). What aspects of the Greek temperament was the Duce not counting on? What does Corelli's enjoyment of the story reveal about him?

Looking over Chapter 24

QUESTIONS FOR ESSAYS OR DISCUSSION

1.   After the bleakness of the Guercio and Mandras stories, Captain Corelli's introduction to the narrative brings with it a fresh comedy and vitality. Assess how the mood of the novel changes, and examine in detail how de Bernières creates this shift in mood in Chapter 24.

2. 'I grew to love him as much as I had loved Francesco, but in an entirely different way.' Compare what Guercio says about Corelli in this chapter with his account of his love for Francesco in Chapter 4 (pp. 40–2).

CHAPTER 25
(pp. 197–208)

Focus on: the Italians

— 'The Italians had turned out to be the modest kind of Romeo that is resigned to being rebuffed, but does not abandon hope' (p. 198). The Cephallonians had expected a different kind of occupying army: 'fathers who expected to be beaten to death stroked the hair of pretty daughters who expected to be raped' (p. 176). What are your impressions of the way the Italians play the role of conquerors? How does de Bernières make them appealing to the reader?

Focus on: altered perspectives

— We already know that Guercio is strong, but, now he is viewed by Pelagia, for the first time we see him in a new perspective: 'He was huge, as big as Velisarios' (pp. 201–2). Whereas Velisarios's reputation as 'the strongest man who had ever lived' (p. 20) was foregrounded from the outset, de Bernières has until now emphasised Guercio's vulnerability. What is the effect of revealing only at this point that Guercio is so physically powerful?
— 'What a man he is. He has a Greek bullet in his leg to show for it' (p. 202). What ironies are at play here?
— Why do you think de Bernières has chosen to associate Corelli with Guercio in this important scene?

Focus on: tensions

TRANSFORM . . .

— Rewrite the narrative around the dialogue between Dr Iannis and Corelli so that it becomes a confrontation not over who occupies Cephallonia, but over who occupies Pelagia's heart. Can the original scene be interpreted in this way?

Looking over Chapter 25

QUESTIONS FOR ESSAYS OR DISCUSSION

1. This chapter presents the confrontation of the conquered and the conquering with ironic humour. Consider the presentation in this chapter of the power of humour and grace to defuse anger and fear.

2. How does de Bernières give a sense of Pelagia's attraction to Corelli in this chapter?

CHAPTER 26
(pp. 209–17)

Focus on: Pelagia and Corelli

COMMENT . . .

— Why does Pelagia send Lemoni away? Is her stated reason the whole truth? Analyse her reactions to Corelli in this chapter.

Focus on: 'all that was gone'

EXPLAIN . . .

— Read the conversation between Pelagia and Mandras on pp. 213–14. Explain why they feel about each other as they do at this moment.

Focus on: rival lovers

CONTRAST . . .
— Compare Corelli's appreciation of the waistcoat with Mandras's. What do their contrasting reactions reveal about the two men?

Looking over Chapter 26

QUESTIONS FOR ESSAYS OR DISCUSSION
1. 'Symmetry is for God, not for us' (p. 216). What does Corelli mean by this? How does his comment relate to the concerns of the novel as a whole?

2. 'Mandras aspires to ideals; Corelli likes people.' Discuss.

CHAPTER 27
(pp. 218–27)

Focus on: music

CONSIDER . . .
— 'She realised suddenly that there was something about music that had never been revealed to her before . . . it was, to those who understood it, an emotional and intellectual odyssey . . . she wanted to share the journey' (p. 224). Consider the part that the mandolin plays in bringing Pelagia and Corelli closer to each other. Why has de Bernières made his romantic hero a musician, do you think?

Focus on: word choice

ANALYSE . . .

— Reread the paragraph starting "'I doubt it," said the captain . . .', and list all of the words that refer to parts of the mandolin. Then list the words referring to the materials it is made out of. Finally, list all of the adjectives. How many of these words are unusual? How many sound beautiful? How does the choice of words convey an impression of the mandolin as a beautifully made instrument?

Looking over Chapter 27

QUESTIONS FOR ESSAYS OR DISCUSSION

1. 'Music and dreams speak the language of the heart.' Discuss.

2. Examine the effect that Corelli has had on Pelagia by the end of this chapter. How aware is she of her feelings for him?

CHAPTER 28
(pp. 228–34)

Focus on: national stereotypes

DISCUSS . . .

— Analyse how the British are stereotyped in this chapter.

Focus on: emotive language

ANALYSE . . .

— Discuss the techniques de Bernières uses to manipulate the reader's reactions to the murder of the old man.

Focus on: the psychology of evil

EXAMINE LANGUAGE . . .

— At several points in the novel de Bernières explores the psychology of evil through characters who commit atrocities. Examine Hector's value system in this chapter. Look also at the way Mandras's thinking degenerates in this chapter. What attitudes and distortions underpin the psychology of these two men as they murder the old man?

Focus on: abuse of language

COMPARE AND REFLECT . . .

— 'The attaching of resonant names to lofty concepts': reread the passage on pp. 232–3, from 'The partisan went inside . . .' to '. . . "historical necessity."' Underline the words and phrases that Hector and Mandras use to justify the brutal murder of the old man. Now read the encyclopaedia entry on Fascism by Mussolini, reproduced in the Contexts section of this guide, and identify the words that he uses to justify Fascism. Are there similarities in how they manipulate language? Reflect on the part that the manipulation of language plays in sustaining any extreme and inhumane ideology, regardless of its political orientation.

Looking over Chapter 28

QUESTIONS FOR ESSAYS OR DISCUSSION

1. 'The psychology of evil is built upon lies.' Discuss.

2. 'Mandras is a victim.' Discuss.

CHAPTER 29
(pp. 235–7)

Focus on: juxtaposition

COMPARE . . .
— This chapter treats some of the themes of the previous chapter – etiquette, guilt, the misuse of language, physical violence, mutual respect – but this time in an ironically humorous way. Compare the moods of the two chapters. What effects are created by their juxtaposition?

Looking over Chapter 29

QUESTION FOR ESSAYS OR DISCUSSION
1. 'The essence of comedy is that it renders malice harmless.' Discuss, with reference to this chapter.

CHAPTER 30
(pp. 238–45)

Focus on: ideas and reality

CONNECT . . .
— How are the allusions to Josiah Tucker connected with the novel's theme of replacing reality with ideas?

Focus on: titles

ANALYSE . . .
— The title 'Nazi' continues to have strong emotive associations. What ideas do you associate with this word? How does de Bernières use Nazi stereotypes? What does the word 'good' seem to mean in the context of 'Nazi'? Considering Weber's portrayal in this chapter, is the title wholly ironic?

Focus on: Weber

COMPARE . . .
— Study Weber's portrayal in this chapter. What hints are there that he is an 'ingenuous and friendly' young man under his stiff manner? Compare his way of speaking and his attitude to the prostitutes with Corelli's.

Focus on: language

TRANSFORM . . .
— Read the description of the prostitutes on pp. 241–2, from 'One would have described . . .' to '. . . the browsing fish that ate them.' What attitude towards the women does this portrayal imply? Rewrite the passage *using only what is already there*, but leaving out whatever you wish, to emphasise the elements of unpleasant reality in their portrayal. Then rewrite it again using the same technique to emphasise the idea of an attractive ideal. Identify the key words in each description. Finally, consider what this exercise reveals about how de Bernières combines these two elements throughout his portrayal.

Looking over Chapter 30

QUESTION FOR ESSAYS OR DISCUSSION
1. Discuss the presentation of uniformity and individuality in this chapter, and relate your observations to how these ideas have been developed in the novel so far.

CHAPTER 31
(pp. 246–53)

Focus on: points of view

INFER . . .

— This chapter presents the developing flirtation between Pelagia and Corelli from her point of view. Read through the chapter again and infer what his view of her is at each stage in the chapter. What effect is created by the sole focus on her view of events?

Focus on: comedy and motive

ANALYSE . . .

— Compare what Pelagia *wants* to feel towards Corelli with what she *actually* feels. How does de Bernières create comedy from this conflict?

Looking over Chapter 31

QUESTIONS FOR ESSAYS OR DISCUSSION

1.   'Throughout the novel, love is seen to spring from the heart, whereas hatred is manufactured in the mind.' Discuss the validity of this claim, with reference to this chapter and to earlier incidents.

2.   'I won, I won.' What has Corelli won, and what hints are there that he is enjoying the battle?

CHAPTER 32
(pp. 254–6)

Focus on: characterisation

IDENTIFY . . .
— Find the details that expose the depth of Mandras's ignorance in this chapter.
— Identify the ways in which Hector manipulates Mandras.

Focus on: context

RESEARCH AND COMPARE . . .
De Bernières alludes to Lenin, and to the text *What Is To Be Done?* Lenin (1870–1924) was a Russian revolutionary politician and theorist, and the founder of Soviet Communism. In *What Is To Be Done?* (1902), he argued that the working masses must be led through a disciplined party organisation by a 'vanguard' of educated professionals. His interpretation of Marx became the official Soviet doctrine after Lenin's death, but it was distorted to justify Stalin's dictatorial regime.
— Research Lenin's theories in more detail. In what ways is Hector's behaviour a distortion of Leninism?
— How do these allusions to Leninism contribute to the novel's theme of the dangers posed by ideologies?

Looking over Chapter 32

QUESTIONS FOR ESSAYS OR DISCUSSION
1. We read earlier that Hector was 'astute enough to see that Mandras was a lost soul' (p. 230). Considering both this chapter and Chapter 28, discuss in what senses Mandras is more 'lost' now than he was before he met Hector.

2. 'Labelling people only hides the truth about them.' Discuss, with reference to this chapter and to Chapter 30.

CHAPTER 33
(pp. 257–62)

Focus on: *the language of euphemism*

READ CLOSELY . . .

— Consider the passage describing Corelli's erotic daydreams on pp. 258–60, from 'Pelagia laughed in malicious glee . . .' to '. . . succulent fruit.' Underline all of the euphemisms that are used, including the images that suggest erotic connotations in this context without being explicitly sexual. Graphic descriptions of sex have been unexceptional in fiction since the 1960s, so the euphemisms are a stylistic choice. Why has de Bernières used euphemism to describe Corelli's excitement and thoughts, do you think? How would the effect created be different if the euphemisms were replaced by explicit description?

Focus on: *mind v. heart*

DISCUSS . . .

— How does de Bernières imply in this chapter that Pelagia and Corelli's rational attempts to discipline their instinctive feelings are a lost cause?

Focus on: *Dr Iannis*

INFER . . .

— Dr Iannis is a silent presence for much of this scene, to the extent that we might easily forget (as, perhaps, do the lovers) that he is there at all. Why has de Bernières included him in the scene, do you think? What does his presence add?

Looking over Chapter 33

QUESTIONS FOR ESSAYS OR DISCUSSION

1. What effects does de Bernières create by alternating the narrative thread of Pelagia and Corelli with that of Mandras?

2. Some of the comedy of this scene depends upon the situation described, and some depends upon the language that is used to describe it. Discuss the comic effects created by each..

CHAPTER 34
(pp. 263–8)

Focus on: national stereotypes

EVALUATE . . .

— Do you find the presentation of the Allies as stereotypes in this chapter effective within the novel's scheme?

Focus on: honour

ASSESS . . .

— What does the idea of 'honour' mean to Myers?

Looking over Chapter 34

QUESTIONS FOR ESSAYS OR DISCUSSION

1. We are told that Myers 'had the moral authority of someone who refuses to compromise an ethical principle in the name of an ideal' (p. 264). How has this idea been explored in the novel so far?

2. Myers calls the ELAS 'red Fascists'. In what ways has de

Bernières emphasised the similarities between the Fascist and Communist habits of thinking in the novel?

CHAPTER 35
(pp. 269–78)

Focus on: context

RESEARCH . . .
— Compare this propagandist account of Mussolini's life with a historical biography. How factually accurate does it appear to be?

Focus on: the language of propaganda

READ CLOSELY . . .
— What techniques does this pamphlet use to manipulate a reader's responses? Consider the use of irony and the use of emotive words and images. Choose one paragraph and underline each instance of the above. Analyse the connotations of the words. Assess how the knowledge that this pamphlet is propagandist affects the way you interpret it.

RESEARCH AND COMPARE . . .
— If you do an Internet search on Mussolini, you will not find it hard to trace neo-Fascist websites that carry pro-Mussolini propaganda. Compare the language that is used on such a site with the language used in this chapter.

Looking over Chapter 35

QUESTION FOR ESSAYS OR DISCUSSION
1. Why has de Bernières inserted this pamphlet at this point in the narrative, do you think?

CHAPTER 36
(pp. 279–83)

Focus on: the language of political theory

ANALYSE . . .
— Read the paragraph on p. 280 starting 'Now, comrades, I want to speak to you . . .'. Underline all of the abstract nouns that Hector uses. How many concrete examples does he give? What arguments does he use to back up his claims? How clear and convincing is his speech? If you can find a copy of *What Is To Be Done?*, compare Hector's language with Lenin's. What is being satirised here: the intellectual pretentiousness of a petty gang leader, or the language of political theory itself?

Looking over Chapter 36

QUESTION FOR ESSAYS OR DISCUSSION
1.   Hector talks of standing together and of trust between comrades. How does de Bernières expose the hypocrisy of his words?

CHAPTER 37
(pp. 284–7)

Focus on: men and women

DISCUSS . . .
— Both Dr Iannis and Pelagia draw conclusions about the other sex from this incident. How ironic are they being? Before you decide, consider the social mores of their village as well as their attitude to the opposite sex elsewhere in the novel.

Looking over Chapter 37

QUESTION FOR ESSAYS OR DISCUSSION

1.   In your opinion, was the printing and disseminating of the leaflet by Guercio and Dr Iannis brave, or foolish, or both? Choose two other episodes involving a conflict between bravery and common sense. Comment on the ways in which your chosen episodes present the tension between the two. In your answer you should

● look closely at language used to describe how characters act

● comment on the place of relevant issues such as social conventions, military protocol, and the relationship between the occupying forces and the Greeks.

CHAPTER 38
(pp. 288–91)

Focus on: men and women

DISCUSS . . .
— How does this chapter draw upon stereotypical male and female behaviour for comic effect?

Looking over Chapter 38

QUESTIONS FOR ESSAYS OR DISCUSSION

1.   Corelli sees Pelagia at this moment as 'a proud woman who prosecuted war with hard words and kindnesses'. Discuss whether Corelli idealises Pelagia, here or earlier.

2.   In what ways does Corelli's status as part of the occupying

force and Pelagia's as one of the conquered villagers colour their relationship in this chapter?

CHAPTER 39
(pp. 292–5)

Focus on: the comic and the serious

DISCUSS . . .
— Analyse the combination of the comic and the serious in this chapter. Consider the passages of prophecy: are they a parody of biblical language? Do they have a serious relevance to the theme of evil in the novel? Is Arsenios being mocked by de Bernières, or does he cease to be a comic character in this chapter? Is the final sentence entirely ironic?

Looking over Chapter 39

QUESTIONS FOR ESSAYS OR DISCUSSION
1. Consider what the characterisation of Father Arsenios contributes to the novel. How do his character, the way he is tolerated when a drunk, and his later transformation into a 'prophet' contribute to our impression of life on Cephallonia and of the Cephallonians' attitude to religion?

2. What is the purpose in the novel's scheme of the passages of Arsenios's prophecy?

CHAPTER 40
(pp. 296–7)

Focus on: Pelagia

ANALYSE . . .
— Why does Pelagia continue to deny to Corelli the affection that she has clearly betrayed several times and which no denial can hide? What aspects of her character, of her circumstances and of her gender role prevent her from openly admitting how she feels for him?

Focus on: the power of love

DISCUSS . . .
— 'A problem with eyes . . . hands . . . lips . . .' How does de Bernières create an increasing sense that, whatever their resistance to how they feel, the eventual full expression of love between Pelagia and Corelli is inevitable?

Looking over Chapter 40

QUESTION FOR ESSAYS OR DISCUSSION
1. When Corelli mockingly plays the part of a spurned lover, his histrionics have the effect of both hiding and revealing how he really feels. In addition to this scene, choose two more scenes in which characters play a part. Discuss why the character plays a part in each, and to what effect.

CHAPTER 41
(pp. 298–302)

Focus on: archetypes

CONSIDER . . .

— '. . . their first unpatriotic and secret kiss' (p. 302). The story of a love that flourishes between enemies, and which must overcome censure or remain secret, is one of the great archetypes of literature. Archetypes have much in common with mythic formulas in stories, and even naturalistic, sophisticated fiction can depend extensively on them for their fictional scheme. Can you think of any other novels, plays or narrative poems that are based on this story? Consider the idea that this novel, although it is set in a realistic, historical time and place, has a significance beyond the time and place in which it is set. How are the main themes made timeless?

Focus on: symbolism

DISCUSS . . .

— Corelli has noted several times that Pelagia smells of rosemary. See if you can find some fresh rosemary to see what he means. It may also have a symbolic quality here: in the language of flowers, rosemary means 'fidelity in love'; in ancient times it was much used in weddings; it was also said to be useful in love-making. Think of other details in the novel so far that lend themselves to a double interpretation, literal and symbolic. What symbolic connotations do the dolphins have, for instance? The mandolin?

Looking over Chapter 41

QUESTION FOR ESSAYS OR DISCUSSION

1. De Bernières has been accused of resorting to romantic

cliché in his depiction of the love between Corelli and Pelagia. In this chapter, how does de Bernières temper a clichéd situation with realism and humour?

CHAPTER 42
(pp. 303–7)

Focus on: conceit

DISCUSS . . .

— The extended comparison between a mandolin and a woman is a kind of post-metaphysical conceit: an unlikely comparison developed through increasingly unlikely stages, more striking for its playfulness and ingenuity than for its truthfulness. Is the playfulness here Corelli's or de Bernières's? What does this comparison add to our impressions of Corelli's character?

Looking over Chapter 42

QUESTION FOR ESSAYS OR DISCUSSION

1. 'I am a man who lacks the courage to take an evil by the throat and throttle it' (p. 306). Is Corelli lacking in courage, in your opinion?

CHAPTER 43
(pp. 308–21)

Focus on: natural law

CONNECT . . .

— 'She was saddened by the cruelty of a world in which the living can only live by predation on creatures weaker than themselves; it seemed a poor way to order a universe' (p. 310). Pelagia's kindly and comic sympathy for snails may have a wider significance: the natural law of the survival of the fittest was often used by Fascists as justification for the moral right of the superior races to oppress those they saw as inferior (Weber articulates this idea on p. 350). Where else in the novel has this idea been expressed?

Focus on: language

ANALYSE . . .
— Read the description of the explosion on pp. 315–17, from 'There was a sharp crack . . .' to '. . . filling up their wrinkles.' The style changes during this passage. Analyse how the grammar, the word combinations and the vocabulary are used to create a sense of an altered reality.

Looking over Chapter 43

QUESTION FOR ESSAYS OR DISCUSSION
1.   'He charged Corelli for acting on his own initiative without permission, for not handing over the responsibility to the qualified authority, for reckless endangerment, and for conduct unbecoming to an officer' (p. 319). In the novel's fictional scheme, does the anarchy that Corelli unleashes in this chapter increase or diminish our opinion of him? Account for your answer.

CHAPTER 44
(pp. 322–6)

Focus on: surprise

COMMENT . . .
— 'She had never dreamed that her captain could have been so cruel, so remorseless' (p. 325). Do you share Pelagia's surprise at Corelli's reaction?

Focus on: the goat

ACCOUNT FOR . . .
— What part has the goat played in the novel so far? Account for Pelagia's reaction (and her fury with Corelli) when it is stolen.

Looking over Chapter 44

QUESTION FOR ESSAYS OR DISCUSSION
1. What does this chapter add to the theme of honour in the novel so far?

CHAPTER 45
(pp. 327–31)

Focus on: Arcadia

RESEARCH AND COMPARE . . .
— The title recalls stories of a golden time of lost innocence which occur in most cultures. The Greek version is Arcadia, a mountainous state in the Peloponnese that was traditionally seen as the home of pastoral simplicity and bliss. Look up 'pastoral' and 'the golden age' in the glossary of literary terms and compare the descriptions with this chapter. How many elements of the archetype are present?

Looking over Chapter 45

QUESTION FOR ESSAYS OR DISCUSSION

1. 'The love between Corelli and Pelagia is a form of escapism.' Discuss.

CHAPTER 46
(pp. 332–9)

Focus on: real Arcadia

CONTRAST . . .

— In what ways does the opening of this chapter (up to 'general direction of the mainland') serve as a counterpoint to the pastoral images of the previous chapter?

Looking over Chapter 46

QUESTION FOR ESSAYS OR DISCUSSION

1. With detailed reference to this chapter, discuss de Bernières's skills as a comic writer.

CHAPTER 47
(pp. 340–8)

Focus on: views on love

EVALUATE . . .

— Dr Iannis: 'I am a doctor and I deal . . . in demonstrable facts' (p. 345). Pelagia: 'You make everything squalid' (p. 347). Evaluate the advice that Dr Iannis gives Pelagia about love. Is it wise? Realistic? Sensitive?

Looking over Chapter 47

QUESTION FOR ESSAYS OR DISCUSSION

1. Discuss Dr Iannis's relationship with Pelagia, with reference to this and to earlier chapters.

CHAPTER 48
(pp. 349–53)

Focus on: morality

ANALYSE . . .

— Compare and contrast Weber's definition of morality with Corelli's. Note that Weber defines morality in abstract terms, whereas Corelli does it through a concrete example. Weber is a 'good Nazi': is Corelli a 'good man' (p. 351)? If so, why? And what does it show about Weber that he can see this?

Looking over Chapter 48

QUESTION FOR ESSAYS OR DISCUSSION

1. 'You're so sweet,' says Pelagia to Weber. How do you react to his character and to his views in this chapter? What part does history after 1941 play in your reaction to him?

CHAPTER 49
(pp. 354–8)

Focus on: Dr Iannis's advice

ANALYSE . . .

— Assess Dr Iannis's attitude to Corelli, and his motives for giving Corelli the 'advice' that he does in this chapter.

84

EVALUATE . . .
— Assess whether Pelagia fits Dr Iannis's description of the Greek temperament.

Focus on: Corelli's reaction

COMMENT . . .
— "'I love her,' said Corelli at last, as though this were the answer to the problem, which to him it was' (p. 358). Comment on what this reaction shows about his character.

Looking over Chapter 49

QUESTION FOR ESSAYS OR DISCUSSION
I.   What does this chapter contribute to the portrayal of national stereotypes in the novel?

CHAPTER 50
(pp. 359–63)

Focus on: mood

ANALYSE . . .
— What is a hiatus? Analyse the ways in which de Bernières creates a sense of a growing mood of apprehension, of something terrible to come, in this and the preceding chapters.

Looking over Chapter 50

QUESTION FOR ESSAYS OR DISCUSSION
I.   Discuss the effect created by the juxtaposition of the account of world events and the domestic scene in this chapter.

CHAPTER 51
(pp. 364–70)

Focus on: narrative voice

INFER . . .
— Why does de Bernières write an account of General Gandin's plight in an imitation of Homer?

Focus on: Corelli

COMMENT . . .
— 'The truth was that he had no home' (p. 370). How does this new aspect of Corelli's character, and the account of what happened to his family, alter our view of him?

Looking over Chapter 51

QUESTION FOR ESSAYS OR DISCUSSION
1.   'De Bernières presents history not as a tragedy, but as a petty confusion of betrayals, incompetence and stupidity.' Discuss, with reference to this and to earlier chapters.

CHAPTER 52
(pp. 371–8)

Focus on: narrative structure

ANALYSE . . .
— How does de Bernières use narrative structure in this chapter to emphasise the effects of decisions by leaders on ordinary people?

Focus on: blame

ANALYSE . . .
— Discuss how this chapter apportions blame for the vulnerability of the Italian soldiers.

Looking over Chapter 52

QUESTION FOR ESSAYS OR DISCUSSION
1. Discuss the theme of betrayal, as it is developed in this chapter.

CHAPTER 53
(pp. 379–82)

Focus on: the exhilaration of battle

READ CLOSELY . . .
— Analyse in detail how de Bernières conveys the experience of engaging in battle on pp. 380–1, from 'The men were exhilarated . . .' to '. . . or getting wed.'

CONNECT AND DISCUSS . . .
— Recall Mandras's 'exhilaration' (p. 232) at beating the old man in Chapter 28, and his realisation that if he 'blocked from his mind the precisely clear picture of what must have been happening' the daughter's wails of grief 'sounded weirdly beautiful' (p. 234). Compare this moral myopia with Appollonio's view of the stricken German landing craft: 'There was a frenzy of activity on the boats that struck him as almost comical, and then he ordered an exact range and gave the command to fire at will' (p. 380). Discuss the claim that lying behind both atrocities is a failure of imagination.

Focus on: blame

WEIGH UP . . .
— 'The battery of Captain Antonio Corelli also opened fire'
(p. 382). How do you react to Corelli's involvement? What does
it illustrate about his character?

Looking over Chapter 53

QUESTION FOR ESSAYS OR DISCUSSION
1.   To what extent does the account of the unauthorised Italian
attack on the German flotilla implicitly criticise the Italians,
implicitly praise them, or take a neutral view?

CHAPTER 54
(pp. 383–5)

Focus on: Guercio

DISCUSS . . .
— What is Guercio's view of himself in this letter?

Looking over Chapter 54

QUESTION FOR ESSAYS OR DISCUSSION
1.   Consider the balance between the emotive manipulation of
the reader and authorial restraint in this chapter. Does de
Bernières get the balance right?

CHAPTER 55
(pp. 386–93)

Focus on: authorial anger

DISCUSS . . .

— 'Cephallonia was an island of no strategic importance, its little children need not be saved, its ancient and buckled buildings need not be preserved for posterity, its blood and flesh were not precious to those conducting a war from easy and Olympian heights' (p. 391). Discuss the techniques that de Bernières uses to convey his anger in this chapter. Do you find them effective?

Looking over Chapter 55

QUESTIONS FOR ESSAYS OR DISCUSSION

1. 'The unspeakable enormity of this war suddenly broke his heart' (p. 391). Explain what is meant by 'unspeakable enormity' in this sentence.

2. Discuss de Bernières's presentation of 'tragedy' (p. 390) in this chapter, and relate it to the theme of tragedy throughout the novel.

CHAPTER 56
(pp. 394–400)

Focus on: abnegation of responsibility

ANALYSE . . .

— Compare the way that the major 'reasoned with himself that since the order came originally from the top, it was Colonel

Barge's responsibility, or perhaps that of someone in Berlin' (p. 395) with Mandras's thought as he kills the old man that 'it was Hector who was the executioner, and he was only the hand. The man had been sentenced to death, and was going to die anyway' (p. 233). In what way does Weber's decision to carry out the execution order differ from the Major's reasoning?

Focus on: forgiveness

DISCUSS . . .

— Does Weber deserve forgiveness? Look at the contrasting attitudes of Corelli and Guercio on p. 397. Which attitude do you admire more?

RESEARCH . . .

— Read a self-help book like, for instance, Johann Christoph Arnold's *Why Forgive?* (Plough Publishing House, Farrington, PA, 2000). How might this relate to Carlo and Corelli's situation in relation to Günter Weber?

Focus on: 'divine madness'

EXPLAIN . . .

— In one sense, Guercio's act of guarding Corelli was not self-sacrifice, since he would have died just the same had he not guarded Corelli. But it is an act of love, filled with 'divine madness'. What does this phrase mean in this context?

Looking over Chapter 56

QUESTIONS FOR ESSAYS OR DISCUSSION

1. Discuss the presentation of Weber in this chapter.

2. Relate the treatment of guilt in this chapter to the development of this theme in the rest of the novel.

CHAPTER 57
(pp. 401–6)

Focus on: apocalyptic images

COMMENT . . .
— Read the description of the pyre on pp. 402–5, from 'Down in the valleys . . .' to '. . . shrivel in the flames.' Pick out the apocalyptic images. What is the effect of Father Arsenios's angry tirade in this context?

Focus on: word choice

DISCUSS . . .
— The Italian soldiers are referred to throughout this chapter as 'boys', a word that might seem incongruous for men such as Guercio. Discuss the effect of the use of this word in this context.

Looking over Chapter 57

QUESTIONS FOR ESSAYS OR DISCUSSION
1. 'The power of this episode is heightened greatly by the reminder that it happened.' Discuss.

2. Select and comment on three details in this chapter that, to you, convey most eloquently the inhumanity of the characters who committed this atrocity.

CHAPTER 58
(pp. 407–16)

Focus on: the obsequy

ANALYSE THE LANGUAGE . . .

— Dr Iannis's obsequy moves into a different register. Analyse the aspects of lexis and grammar that create this register.

DISCUSS . . .

— Dr Iannis quotes some sayings of conventional wisdom. Discuss what each of them means.

— 'Nothing can harm a good man, either in life or after death' (p. 415). Guercio's life seems to repudiate this. In what sense might it nevertheless be true?

Looking over Chapter 58

QUESTIONS FOR ESSAYS OR DISCUSSION

1. Dr Iannis twice performs the role of religious minister in this chapter, and he also ministers as a doctor to Corelli. Pagan and materialist though he claims to be, in what sense can he be described as a spiritual man?

2. Guercio is buried like a mythical Greek hero. Discuss the ways in which he is a heroic character.

CHAPTER 59
(pp. 417–20)

Focus on: descriptive technique

ANALYSE THE LANGUAGE . . .
— How effectively does de Bernières convey Corelli's physical pain in this chapter? Analyse how he builds up the description.

Looking over Chapter 59

QUESTION FOR ESSAYS OR DISCUSSION
1. 'The truth will make us free.' Consider the themes of truth-telling and lying in the novel so far.

CHAPTER 60
(pp. 421–7)

Focus on: the passage of time

DISCUSS . . .
— There are several details in this chapter that link the events of the 1940s to the present. Read the passage on p. 422 from 'There was always the sea . . .' to '. . . without acknowledgement or a word.' What does this allusion to today imply about our relationship with the past?

Focus on: caricature

CONSIDER . . .
— Does the caricature of Bunny Warren fit successfully with the mood of the rest of this chapter?

Looking over Chapter 60

QUESTION FOR ESSAYS OR DISCUSSION

1. 'There is always a choice' (p. 423) says Pelagia. Consider the choice that Pelagia makes to arrange Corelli's removal from the island. Then discuss this and two more important choices in the novel, analysing what each reveals about the character who makes it.

CHAPTER 61
(pp. 428–37)

Focus on: allusion

COMPARE AND CONTRAST . . .

— Read Shakespeare's *Romeo and Juliet* and compare the two love scenes in the play – Act II, scene 2 and Act III, scene 5 – with the scene between Corelli and Pelagia as they say goodbye. Note how, in both cases, the subjects discussed by the lovers are similar: how they love each other, what they will do when they get together again, how they will remember this moment, how social or political circumstances have conspired to part them. Try to find as many examples of similarity as you can.
— Then look at the language used. Again, in what ways is it the same and in what ways is it different? Consider also the relevance of de Bernieres's chapter heading. How might that indicate an allusion to Shakespeare?

Looking over Chapter 61

QUESTIONS FOR ESSAYS OR DISCUSSION

1. Consider the ways in which death is imaged and referred to in this Chapter.

2. What is the significance of Doctor Iannis's role in this scene?

CHAPTERS 62 AND 63
(pp. 438–53)

Focus on: contrasts and irony, friends and enemies

ANALYSE . . .

— Consider the tone of Chapter 62 compared with that of Chapter 63. In a slightly teasing and yet rueful way the narrator explains how there came to be a turnaround in the attitudes of the islanders to the two different armies who occupied Cephallonia. In retrospect, and compared with the occupying German army, the Italians began to seem no more than lovable rogues, in spite of the fact that they had once been the enemy. Pick out words and phrases that moderate the picture of the Italians, and then pick out the words and phrases that condemn the Germans.

— Then look at Chapter 63 where the story moves from the larger scene of the whole island's experience to the events surrounding Mandras's return. He was once a friend – now he has become the enemy. Look for the key words and phrases that condemn him.

COMPARE AND CONTRAST . . .

— As you read pp. 451–3 which tell of the death of Mandras, look back at Chapter 11 (pp. 75–83) and consider the ironies in what he was, compared with what he had become.

Looking over Chapters 62 and 63

QUESTIONS FOR ESSAYS OR DISCUSSION

1. 'Mandras is a victim of circumstances'. Discuss.

2. 'There are only women and soldiers'. Discuss.

3. 'The true enemy is always within'. Discuss in relation to these chapters.

4. Do you approve of Drosoula's actions in this section? Why? Why not?

5. De Bernières's tone is light, his subject matter is serious. Is this jokey style an appropriate way in which to write about weighty matters?

6. Consider the ways in which de Bernières uses the island of Cephallonia as an image of the larger Europe engulfed in war.

7. Write on Gunter Weber's role in this part of the novel.

CHAPTER 64
(pp. 454–62)

Focus on: naming

EXPLAIN . . .
— Pelagia's adopted daughter is called Antonia. But she also ends up getting called Psipsina. Work through the various Antonios and Antonias in the novel, and through the

various Psipsinas. Then explain a) the logical relations of each one to the other, and b) the metaphorical and symbolic relations of each one to the other.

Looking over Chapter 64

QUESTION FOR ESSAYS OR DISCUSSION
1. Describe the roles of the children in this novel.

CHAPTERS 65 AND 66
(pp. 462–77)

Focus on: the treatment of history

DEFINE AND ILLUSTRATE . . .
— If you look at the interview with de Bernières you will see that he says that it was the story of the earthquake that began his interest in the history of Cephallonia. You will also remember that the Doctor was supposed to be writing the definitive history of the island. And that beyond that 'real' history, and the Doctor's subjective history, there is the mythical history where *Captain Corelli's Mandolin* can be read as a revision of Homer's *Odyssey*. Discriminate the places where these different types of history are being employed in the novel.

Looking over Chapters 65 and 66

QUESTIONS FOR ESSAYS OR DISCUSSION
1. 'History is an untruth'. Discuss.

2. 'Man does, woman is'. Is this a fair account of what happens in the novel?

3.   How does the fact of the earthquake in Cephallonia relate to the themes of the novel as a whole?

4.   In what ways does the Doctor 'find his voice' in the novel as a whole?

5.   Examine the language of break up and decay used in these chapters.

6.   How well (or otherwise) do the various assisting nations come out of de Bernières's account of the earthquake in Cephallonia?

CHAPTER 67
(pp. 478–80)

Focus on: forms of tragedy

RESEARCH AND COMPARE . . .
— Ancient Greek tragedy had, for the most part, a rigid formal structure. A Chorus – a group of bystanders not directly involved in the action of the story – would introduce the key elements of the story so far and comment on events as they unfolded. Interspersed with these commentaries come long soliloquies by the principals as they consider their situation and choices, and sometimes dialogue between two of the principals that will move events along. Pelagia's Lament parallels such patterns in Greek tragedy where the action stops and the character's problems are discussed directly with herself, but also, by implication, with the audience or, in this case, the reader.
— Look for a translation of a Greek tragedy: Euripedes' *Medea* for instance, or Aeschylus's *Agamemnon*, and look particularly at the speeches of Medea and Clytemnestra. Then compare the style of their speeches with this one of Pelagia's.

Looking over Chapter 67

QUESTION FOR ESSAYS OR DISCUSSION
1. Who, in your own view, is the most important character in *Captain Corelli's Mandolin*?

CHAPTERS 68 AND 69
(pp. 481–96)

Focus on: connections

REVIEW AND COMPARE . . .
— Many strands in the novel begin to be brought together now. Look over these two chapters and count how many you can find. Some are within these two chapters – for instance Antonia's attitude towards the king expressed in Chapter 68, and her reaction to his death in the next chapter. Others refer back to scenes that appeared much earlier – the proverb in the heading to Chapter 69, for instance, is something we had encountered in a scene between Corelli and Pelagia.
— Note also that two different 'histories' are being constructed here. Pelagia takes up the 'personal history' of the island that her father had begun, while a new story is being composed by the arrival of the sequence of mysterious postcards from abroad. Why do you suppose that de Bernières has set these two stories side by side? Which is to do with the past? And which is to do with the future?

Looking over Chapters 68 and 69

QUESTIONS FOR ESSAYS OR DISCUSSION
1. Assess the ways in which the Doctor's history of

99

Cephallonia figures as a patterning device in the novel as a whole.

2. Should Pelagia feel guilty?

3. Analyse the theme of voyaging away from home in this section.

4. 'Everything connected to everything else in the most elaborate, devious, and elegant ways' (p. 486). How might this statement be read as a motto for *Captain Corelli's Mandolin*?

CHAPTERS 70, 71 AND 72
(pp. 497–517)

Focus on: the theme of storytelling

COUNT AND ASSESS . . .
— How many stories told in these chapters are actually re-tellings of events that we have already heard in the course of the novel? What do you suppose is the purpose of this recapitulation?

Looking over Chapters 70, 71 and 72

QUESTIONS FOR ESSAYS OR DISCUSSION
1. 'History repeats itself, first as tragedy, and then again as tragedy' (p. 441). Consider this remark in the light of the novel as a whole.

2. Analyse the use of music in *Captain Corelli's Mandolin*.

3. Consider the ways in which de Bernières uses myth and legend in this novel.

CHAPTER 73
(pp. 518–33)

Focus on: endings

ASK YOURSELF . . .

— Pelagia says, 'I feel like an unfinished poem' (p. 520). What do you think she means?

— When Pelagia points out to Corelli that the child he had seen her with may have been the result of rape, he admits that it would have 'made a difference'. That is, he would have hesitated about marrying her. He adds, 'Thank God we are not so stupid now. Some things change for the better'. What do you think about Corelli's old attitude?

CONSIDER MEMENTOES AND GIFTS . . .

— Corelli shows Pelagia two things to remind her of their past together: the handkerchief stained with her blood, and the embroidered waistcoat that she had made. Look back over the novel and assess the significance of these items in terms of the unfolding of their relationship.

— Corelli also gives Pelagia three things on three consecutive days. Where else might you find three gifts given over three days? That is, in what sort of story? Then consider each one of those gifts: the Walkman, the goat, the motorbike hired for two days. What does each one signify a) about the past? And b) about the future?

INTERPRET . . .

— The novel ends with a vision of three girls on a moped. De Bernières talks about this image in the interview. But before you consider that, try and interpret the image for yourself, and assess what it means to Corelli. In what ways does this moment focus the themes and concerns of the novel as a whole?

Looking over Chapter 73

QUESTIONS FOR ESSAYS OR DISCUSSION

1. Is the ending of *Captain Corelli's Mandolin* happy, or unhappy?

2. Assess the theme of 're-building' in this Chapter and in the novel as a whole.

3. 'Lyrical and angry, satirical and earnest'. Which is the best description of *Captain Corelli's Mandolin*?

4. Why is it important to the working out of the themes of the novel that it should cover such a long time span?

Looking over the whole novel

QUESTIONS FOR ESSAYS OR DISCUSSION

1. Consider the theme of love in *Captain Corelli's Mandolin*. How might Pelagia, Dr Iannis, Mandras and Corelli define love? Do any of them live up to his or her ideal?

2. De Bernières has said, 'I always seem to be writing about the abuse of power: what happens to ordinary people when megalomaniacs get busy.' Consider which characters abuse power in *Captain Corelli's Mandolin*, and discuss how de Bernières explores the effects of this abuse on ordinary people.

3. 'Honour and common sense; in the light of the other, both of them are ridiculous' (p. 393). Does the novel as a whole support this statement?

4. The novelist A. S. Byatt has written about de Bernières's

'fierce moral rigour'. Define the moral perspective of *Captain Corelli's Mandolin*.

5.   Discuss the theme of music and song in *Captain Corelli's Mandolin*.

6.   'Cephallonia . . . is an island so immense in antiquity that the very rocks themselves exhale nostalgia and the red earth lies stupefied not only by the sun, but by the impossible weight of memory' (p. 5). How is the Cephallonians' view of themselves shaped by their sense of the island's past?

7.   Consider how the Cephallonians view their occupiers and conquerors. In what ways does their history colour their attitudes?

8.   One critic has commented that, for de Bernières, 'heroes are those, of whatever race, who have the moral authority of someone who refuses to compromise an ethical principle in the name of an ideal, and who allow friendship to survive the most extreme tests'. Discuss Dr Iannis and Guercio in the light of this comment.

9.   What does *Captain Corelli's Mandolin* say about political ideology?

10.   '*Captain Corelli's Mandolin* does not shirk from evil or trivialise it, but remains optimistic in the face of it.' Through a discussion of three episodes, consider de Bernières's handling of the theme of evil in the novel.

11.   *Captain Corelli's Mandolin* retells history through many voices. Discuss the effects that de Bernières creates with this narrative method.

12. Discuss de Bernières's presentation of real historical events in the novel.

13. Many of the novel's characters are compared with figures from Greek mythology. What does the novel imply about time and its effects through these comparisons?

14. Choose three episodes from *Captain Corelli's Mandolin* and discuss them as examples of de Bernières's imagination for detail. In your answer you should

- look closely at language and narrative method
- comment on the place of issues such as the social attitudes and habits that govern the characters you are discussing.

Contexts, Comparisons, and Complementary Readings

CAPTAIN CORELLI'S MANDOLIN

These sections suggest contextual and comparative ways of reading these novels by de Bernières. You can put your reading in a social, historical or literary context. You can make comparisons – again, social, literary or historical – with other texts or art works. Or you can choose complementary works (of whatever kind) – that is, art works, or literary works, or social reportage, or facts which in some way illuminate the text by sidelights or interventions which you can make into a telling framework. Some of the suggested contexts are directly connected to the book, in that they will give you precise literary or social frames in which to situate the novel. In turn, these are either related to the period within which the novel is set, or to the time – now – when you are reading it. Some of these examples are designed to suggest books or other texts that may make useful sources for comparison (or for complementary purposes) when you are reading *Captain Corelli's Mandolin*. Again, they may be related to literary or critical themes, or they may be relevant to social and cultural themes current 'then' or 'now'.

Focus on: the theme of history and political manipulation

COMPARE . . .

Read these extracts. The first is from the Italian Encyclopaedia. It is a definition of fascism written by Benito Mussolini in 1932. The second is an extract from the beginning of an open letter to Adolf Hitler written by M. Georges Vlachos and published in the *Kathimerini* on March 8th 1941. It is about the position of Greece in relation to her treatment by the occupying forces of Italy and, later, Germany. In what ways are Mussolini's historical ideas about fascist doctrine played out in *Captain Corelli's Mandolin*? And how does Vlachos's letter help you to place the events portrayed in the novel?

In 1932 Mussolini wrote an entry for the Italian Encyclopaedia on the definition of fascism.

Fascism, the more it considers and observes the future and the development of humanity quite apart from political considerations of the moment, believes neither in the possibility nor the utility of perpetual peace. It thus repudiates the doctrine of Pacifism – born of a renunciation of the struggle and an act of cowardice in the face of sacrifice. War alone brings up to its highest tension all human energy and puts the stamp of nobility upon the peoples who have courage to meet it. All other trials are substitutes, which never really put men into the position where they have to make the great decision – the alternative of life or death . . .

. . . After Socialism, Fascism combats the whole complex system of democratic ideology, and repudiates it, whether in its theoretical premises or in its practical application. Fascism denies that the majority, by the simple fact that it is a majority, can direct human society; it denies that numbers alone can govern by means of a periodical consultation, and it affirms the immutable, beneficial, and fruitful inequality of mankind, which can never be permanently levelled through the mere operation of a mechanical process such as universal suffrage . . .

. . . Fascism denies, in democracy, the absurd conventional untruth of political equality dressed out in the garb of collective irresponsibility, and the myth of 'happiness' and indefinite progress . . .

. . . The Fascist State organises the nation, but leaves a sufficient margin of liberty to the individual; the latter is deprived of all useless and possibly harmful freedom, but retains what is essential; the deciding power in this question cannot be the individual, but the State alone . . .

. . . For Fascism, the growth of empire, that is to say the expansion of the nation, is an essential manifestation of vitality, and its opposite a sign of decadence . . . But empire demands discipline, the co-ordination of all forces and a deeply felt sense of duty and sacrifice: this fact explains many aspects of the practical working of the regime, the character of many forces in the State, and the necessarily severe measures which must be taken against those who would oppose this spontaneous and inevitable movement of Italy in the twentieth century, and would oppose it by recalling the outworn ideology of the nineteenth century – repudiated wheresoever there has been the courage to undertake great experiments of social and political transformation; for never before has the nation stood more in need of authority, of direction and order. If every age has its own characteristic doctrine, there are a thousand signs which point to Fascism as the characteristic doctrine of our time. For if a doctrine must be a living thing, this is proved by the fact that Fascism has created a living faith; and that this faith is very powerful in the minds of men is demonstrated by those who have suffered and died for it.

Quoted in the *Internet Modern History Sourcebook*

Translation of an open letter to Hitler from M. Georges Vlakhos, published in the *Kathimerini* of Saturday, March 8th, 1941.

To His Excellency, Adolf Hitler,
Chancellor of the German Reich

Excellency,
Greece, as you know, wished to keep out of the present war. When it broke out she had barely recovered from the wounds that she had suffered from various wars and dissentions at home. She had neither the strength nor the intention, nor any reason to take part in a war, the end of which, no doubt, would be of great importance to the whole world, but at the start did not offer any direct threat to her integrity. Let us ignore her declarations on this point, let us ignore the official documents published in the White Book, let us ignore the speeches and articles which bore witness to her permanent desire to keep out of the war. Let us take into account one fact only. When, after the Italian sinking of the *Elli* in the port of Tinos, Greece found the remains of torpedoes, when she had proof that these torpedoes were Italian, she kept silent. Why? Because if she had disclosed the truth she would have been forced either to declare war, or to see war declared against her. Greece never wished for war with Italy, neither by herself nor with allies, whether these be British or Balkan. She

wished only for her small part of the world to live as quietly as possible, because she was exhausted, because she had fought many wars and because her geographical position is such that she could not have as an enemy either the Germans on land or the English on sea.

At the moment of the sinking of the *Elli*, Greece, apart from her pacific longings, had a guarantee as well, bearing two signatures. The Italian signature, which had guaranteed her against all aggression on the part of Italy, and that of England, which was a spontaneous guarantee of Greek integrity. Nevertheless, when, some time after the sinking of the *Elli*, Italy had shown clearer signs of her future aggression, Greece, convinced that the first signature was valueless, did not turn, as she should have turned, towards the country which had given her the second. She turned – do you remember, Excellency? – towards yourself, and she asked for your protection. What was the reply we were given then? What was said I do not know exactly, but this I know, because I heard it from the lips of our late President himself, that Germany replied to our request by advising us not to offer any pretexts – that is to say, not to mobilise – and to stay quiet.

We did not offer any pretexts, we did not mobilise; we slept quietly, or rather we were sleeping quietly – for that evening the Italians had invited us to dinner – when the Italian Minister appeared with his ultimatum. To whom and where then would you have liked us to turn? Towards Italy, whose valueless signature we had in our pocket with the remains of the torpedoes? But it was the Italians who had declared the war. Towards yourself? But unfortunately that very morning of October 28th, you were in Florence. To remain alone? We had no air force, no material, no money and no fleet. We turned then to the signature left, to the English. And those whose own homeland was in flames, those were keeping anxious watch and ward on the Channel, those who, they said it themselves, had not sufficient material for their own defence, they came, and they came immediately. Without haggling, without excuses, they came, and a few days later on the front in the mountains of Epirus, where the brutal Italian aggression had begun, fell together the Greek troops and the first English airman.

What happened after that you know well, you and the whole world. The Italians have been thrashed. They have been thrashed there man to man by us, the weak and feeble Greeks. Not by the English, because no English soldier has set foot in Albania. The Italians have been thrashed. Why? Because they had no ideals, because they had no heart in the fight, because – but this is another story. In the face of this victory, it is sure because we have been told so, you have remained a spectator. 'This affair,' you said, 'does not interest me. It concerns the Italians only. I will only interfere when the English army lands at Salonika in numbers.' We could have asked your Excellency: 'Florence? Is it a fact that on the very day that the Italians attacked us you were meeting them on the banks of the Arno, and you handed over to them the Greeks?' But we did not wish to ask. Hidden away with the remains of the Italian torpedoes we hid Florence also, and when indiscreet people brought it to our notice we said, 'They were not in agreement, the Italians deceived them.' Why?

Because that is what we wished to believe. That is what it was our interest to believe. So at the same time as we were advancing in Albania, our relations with Germany went smoothly on their way. The swastika flew from your Legation on New Year's day, it came to half-mast when Metaxas dies, and your Minister paid his respects to the new President of the Council. Commercial dealings were renewed, and you yourselves protested strongly on one occasion when an American paper announced that German tanks had appeared in Albania. You as spectators, and the English, our allies, with their air force and their fleet. Only that. You know how we tried to keep that 'Only that' a reality. Enough to say that when an English aeroplane crashed at Salonika we asked the English not to salvage it themselves, in order that not even ten British soldiers should appear there, in order that there should be no misunderstanding, no pretexts. You laugh? How right you are . . .

But enough. Forget the past. Come to facts. According to every witness station in the world it appears that the Germans wished to invade Greece. Why? If an attack on Greece was from the beginning essential to the interests of the Axis, M. Grazzi would not have been alone four months ago at three o'clock in the morning. Germany and Italy would have been together. From the beginning, therefore, the attack on Greece does not seem to have been necessary for the Axis. Apparently now it is. But why? Is it an order that a front was not to be created in the Balkans against Germany? But this comes out of a fairy story. Neither the Greeks nor the English — this was stated officially in a communiqué of March 6th, and is shouted from the housetops by logic — nor Serbia nor Turkey have any reason for spreading the war. The war as it has been is big enough for all these countries. Is it, then, in order to save the Italians in Albania? But what sort of salvation is this? The Italians have been thrashed openly and for all eternity, and will not the public opinion of the world

III

be certain of this thrashing as soon as a single German soldier steps on to the soil of Greece? Will not the whole world shout that forty-five millions of Italians after having attacked our poor eight millions, have now to call for help to another eighty-five millions? But if the Italians wish to be saved, why should others come to their help in a way which is particularly humiliating for them when we could save them ourselves with pleasure and without exposing them to ridicule? Let the Italians evacuate Albania, let them shout from the housetops that they are tired of chasing us and are satiated with glory and have decided to retire. We will help them. But, Excellency, perhaps you are going to say to us, 'This is all very well, but what about the English?'

But it is not we, your Excellency, who made the English come to Greece. It was the Italians. And now you wish us to say farewell to those whom the Italians brought here. So be it. Let us say it. But to whom? To the living. But how can we throw out the dead? Those who died on our mountains. Those who, wounded, fell to earth in Attica and drew there their last breath. Those who at a time when their own country was in flames came to Greece and fought there, died there, and there found their graves. Listen, your Excellency, there are deeds which cannot be done in Greece, and that is one of them. We cannot throw out either the living or the dead. We will throw out no one, but we shall stand here upright by their side until the day when the sunshine breaks through the storm.

Everyone is saying that you intend to invade Greece. But we do not believe it, and we are an ingenuous people. We do not believe it of your army, with its history and its traditions which even its enemies do not deny. We do not believe that your army is willing to

. . . that Fascist Italy dared measure herself against Great Britain is a matter of pride that will live through the centuries. It was an act of conscious daring. People become great by daring, risking and suffering, and not by placing themselves by the wayside in parasitic and vile expectancy. The protagonists of history can revindicate their rights, but simple spectators never can.

Tenth, to beat the Axis, Great Britain's armies would have to land on the Continent, invade Germany and Italy and defeat their armies, and this no Englishman, no matter how insane and delirious by the use and abuse of drugs and alcohol, can even dream of.

Let me say now that what is occurring in the United States is one of the most colossal mystifications in all history. Illusion and lying are the basis of American interventionism-illusion that the United States is still a democracy, when instead it is a political and financial oligarchy dominated by Jews, through a personal form of dictatorship. The lie is that the Axis powers, after they finish Great Britain, want to attack America.

Neither in Rome nor Berlin are such fantastic plans as this prepared. These projects could not be made by those who have an inclination for the madhouse. Though we certainly are totalitarian and will always be so, we have our feet on hard ground. Americans who will read what I say should be calm and not believe in the existence of a big bad wolf who wants to devour them.

. . . Rome comrades! Through you I want to speak to the Italian people, to the authentic, real, great Italian people, who fight with the courage of lions on land, sea and air fronts; people who early in the morning are up to go to work in fields, factories and offices; people who do not permit themselves luxuries, not even innocent ones.

They absolutely must not be confused or contaminated by the minority or well-known poltroons, anti-social individuals and complainers, who grumble about rations and regret their suspended comforts, or by snakes, the remains of the Masonic lodges, whom we will crush without difficulties when and how we want.

The Italian people, the Fascist people deserve and will have victory. The hardships, suffering and sacrifices that are faced with exemplary courage and dignity by the Italian people will have their day of compensation when all the enemy forces are crushed on the battlefields by the heroism of our soldiers and a triple, immense cry will cross the mountains and oceans like lightning and light new hopes and give new certainties to spirit multitudes: Victory, Italy, peace with justice among peoples!

RESEARCH . . .

There are a number of real people mentioned in *Captain Corelli's Mandolin*. Some of these are politicians and leaders, like Benito Mussolini, others are soldiers or diplomats. One such is Maurice Cardiff who is mentioned on page 360. You might like to read his book *Friends Abroad* (The Radcliffe Press, London and New York, 1997). Find out about any other real characters that you can discover in the novel and consider what it means to use real historical figures in works of fiction.

Focus on: Greek myth

RESEARCH AND ANALYSE . . .

De Bernières has said that *Captain Corelli's Mandolin* draws on the *Odyssey* of Homer, but there are many other allusions to Greek myth as well. Read a book of Greek myths and consider how many stories you can find that might relate to the events and the images in *Captain Corelli*. In particular you could look at the stories of Penelope, Ulysses, Circe, Apollo, Philoctetes, the Lotus Eaters, Hades, the Titans, Zeno, Poseidon, Zeus and Athene.

Focus on: adaptation

CONTRAST AND COMPARE . . .
Captain Corelli's Mandolin was made into a Miramax film in 2001 directed by John Madden and with a screenplay by Shawn Slovo. See the film or read the screenplay, and consider the differences between the novel and this adaptation. The timescale is changed, the ending is happier, and Carlo's relation to Corelli is made less explicit. What might this tell you about the requirements of the different forms, or about the need to cater to mass audiences?

VINTAGE
LIVING
TEXTS

The War of Don Emmanuel's Nether Parts

IN CLOSE-UP

Reading guides

THE WAR OF DON EMMANUEL'S NETHER PARTS

BEFORE YOU BEGIN TO READ . . .
Look at the interview with de Bernières and read the section on the Latin-American trilogy. You will see there that de Bernières identifies a number of themes including

- Political corruption
- Moral responsibility
- The presentation of character
- Writing about violence
- Magic
- The treatment of history

While you are reading in detail it is worth bearing these overall themes in mind.

CHAPTER I
(pp. 1–9)

Focus on: setting, atmosphere and character

ANALYSE . . .

— In seven short sections we are introduced to seven char-acters including Capitan Rodrigo Jose Figueras, Misael, Profesor Luis, Consuelo, Hectoro, Pedro and Farides. And we are introduced to a strange world. Make two lists: one should consist of all the phrases that describe the place and setting; the other should consist of the phrases that describe the key characteristics of the seven people. Consider how de Bernières has built up the atmosphere and character of this society in this section.

Focus on: openings

COMPARE AND COMMENT ON . . .

— Read the opening chapter of Jane Austen's *Pride and Prejudice* (1813). Both novels begin with a statement starting with 'It . . .'. In de Bernières: 'It had been an auspicious week for Capitan Rodrigo Jose Figuras.' And in Austen: 'It is a truth universally acknowledged, that a single man in possession of a good for-tune, must be in want of a wife.' In each case, evaluate the ways in which the reader is drawn into the text. What is it that encourages you to go on reading? Then define the tone of each of these opening chapters. They are both ironic. Both might be described as 'satire'. Research this literary term and analyse the use of satire in both.

— Although these two novels are set in different places and times, can you find any similarities in subject matter and in the portrayal of values? You might compare, for example, Capitan Rodrigo's attitude to women, with Mrs Bennett's attitude to

her daughters. In what ways are you shown that both characters think of women as 'currency', something with a value of
a kind?

Focus on: the language of irony

EXPLAIN . . .

— There are several phrases used about the Capitan's actions
in the first and last sections of this chapter that alert you to the
topsy-turvy values he possesses and that characterise his society
– 'According to the usual procedure' for instance, or the peasant
offered to 'pay the fine' (p. 1). Look for more examples like this
and explain their ironic impact. You might also like to look at
the opening chapter of George Orwell's novel *Nineteen Eighty-
Four* (1949) to find similar ironic phrases and techniques designed
to describe a less than satisfactory social regime.

CHAPTERS 2, 3 AND 4
(pp. 10–31)

Focus on: storytelling

TRACE . . .

— Each of these three chapter headings begins with 'In
which . . .'. If you turn to the interview with de Bernières, he
describes this method as rather 'eighteenth century' in tone. If
you look at the chapter headings to Henry Fielding's novel *Tom
Jones* (1749) or Lawrence Sterne's *Tristram Shandy* (1759–67), then
you will be able to see the model. This method also works like
certain kinds of fairy-tale titles. Trace the effect of this tone
in these chapters. How would you define the types of literary
genre being used here?

— In the interview with de Bernières, he also says that it is his practice to write each chapter individually and then shuffle them around to arrive at an order. Would it have mattered if these three chapters appeared in a different order?

Focus on: class structures

COMPARE AND CONTRAST . . .

— On pp. 12–16, there is an elaborate list of the various groups that make up the strata of society in this imaginary Latin-American country. Consider the ways in which the differing characters and situations of Dona Constanza, Federico, Sergio and Don Emmanuel relate to the social groups indicated here.

Focus on: myths

RESEARCH . . .

— On p. 29, Don Emmanuel is said to have begun to 'live like Diogenes and labour like Sisyphus'. Look up both these names in a dictionary of classical history and myth, and work out the reference. How does Don Emmanuel live? How does he work? Could you have worked this out from the text, without looking up the references?

Focus on: language

ILLUSTRATE EXAGGERATION AND UNDERSTATEMENT . . .

— When Sergio and his friends go to see Don Emmanuel they engage in playful banter about his attributes. Look up hyperbole in the Glossary of Literary Terms. How does it work here? Can you find other examples in the novel as a whole? Where do you encounter hyperbole in everyday life? Collect some examples.

— The contrary linguistic figure is understatement (or '*meiosis*' in the Greek term, meaning 'lessening', 'making smaller'). Look for examples of understatement in the novel as a whole.

— Read these sayings attributed to the American film director Woody Allen:

- 'It's not that I'm afraid to die. I just don't want to be there when it happens.'
- 'I don't want to achieve immortality through my work . . . I want to achieve it through not dying.'
- 'I recently turned sixty. Practically a third of my life is over.'
- 'It [being bisexual] immediately doubles your chances for a date on Saturday night.'

How would you define these? Are they exaggerations? Or understatements? Or something else altogether? Consider how this kind of humour works. What makes these statements funny? Using the glossary of literary terms, can you describe them by identifying the figures of literary language that are being set to work?

CHAPTER 5
(pp. 32–9)

Focus on: contrasts and parallels

CRITICALLY EVALUATE . . .
'The violence was the first spasm in a civil war that has never truly ended because no one ever understood why it had begun. It is possible to trace its origins in the manner of a historian; but not without becoming confused' (p. 33).
— This chapter sets an attempt at explaining *'la violencia'* – which de Bernières discusses in the interview – against an account of what happens to Remedios and her parents. Justify the paralleling in this method of narration, and analyse the various registers of tone employed here.

CHAPTERS 6 AND 7
(pp. 40–54)

Focus on: contrasts and parallels

OUTLINE . . .
— Chapter 6 includes an ironic account of the political situation, an analysis of patriotism versus nationalism and the delicate matter of negotiating between political affiliations and national interests. Chapter 7 includes the smaller personal story of Don Emmanuel's visit to Dona Constanza, and his manipulation of her reaction to achieve the result he desires. Compare the public story with the private story. In what ways are they the same? What is the impact of this juxtaposition?

CHAPTERS 8 AND 9
(pp. 55–71)

Focus on: individuals and groups

RELATE . . .
— Consider the connections between Aurelio's story in Chapter 8 and Federico's story in Chapter 9. At first both are alone. Compare their experiences. Then both are integrated — in a certain sense — into a group. What is the same about de Bernières's description of the integration process for both these characters? Then look back at Chapter 5 where Remedios was first introduced and compare the story of her isolation and subsequent integration.

CHAPTER 10
(pp. 72–81)

Focus on: characterisation

RETELL . . .

— Tell the story of the encounter between Figueras and Dona Constanza, first of all from his point of view, then from hers. Remember to look back at the beginning of the episode at the end of Chapter 7 on page 54.

CHAPTERS 11 AND 12
(pp. 82–97)

Focus on: scene setting

COMPARE . . .

— Aurelio and Federico are both being educated in these chapters. Compare the two accounts of their experiences. In what ways are they the same? In what ways are they different as a result of the two different settings in the jungle and with the outlaws?

RESEARCH AND COMPARE . . .

— Read the chapters in Evelyn Waugh's *A Handful of Dust* (1934) which tell how Tony Last departs for the Amazon and ends up being rescued by a recluse called Mr Todd who keeps him and condemns him to an indefinite future of reading Dickens aloud. On p. 82 of *Don Emmanuel* we are told that the Navantes are 'hospitable to white people on condition that they never tried to leave'. Compare the two episodes in these two books. How is the image of the jungle treated in each?

Focus on: humour and irony

EXPLAIN . . .

When Aurelio's wives give birth, he undergoes 'the couvade'. 'He took to his hammock for four days at each birth, groaning with the pain of the delivery, to be tended by his anxious spouse, who had given birth squatting over a hole in the ground. In this way the men took away the pain of birth and took it on themselves' (p. 88).

When Garcia is defrocked for fornication – which he did not commit – he persuades himself that he must rescue the soul of the bishop who has committed the sin of condemning an innocent man. 'One morning after fervent prayer Garcia decided to save the bishop's soul by destroying his own innocence and committing the very crime for which he had been condemned . . . he quite possibly believed that by committing the sin as often as possible he made doubly sure of saving the bishop's soul' (p. 91).

— Comment on the impact of these passages. Is there any sense in which they are not funny?

Focus on: characterisation

SUMMARISE . . .

— How do we know that General Fuerte is a good man? What particular elements contribute to that impression? In an irrational and arbitrary world of violence and injustice, how surprising is it – at this late stage – to come across a voice of reason when the General says that he would court-martial soldiers guilty of murder and rape (p. 96)?

CHAPTER 13 AND 14
(pp. 98–115)

Focus on: the theme of war and violence and its effects

COMPARE . . .

— Both of these stories about Tomas and Gonzago and about Parlanchina describe the casualties of civil war, and also the continuing effects as others become involved in the extending circle of violence: '. . . the only reasons that campesinos ever become guerrillas; personal ones' (p. 105). Consider and compare the events of these two stories.

RESEARCH . . .

— Parlanchina dies when she steps on a landmine. Research where and how landmines are still used today, especially in African countries at war with themselves. Children are particularly vulnerable and often lose limbs – if they do not die. The late Diana, Princess of Wales was a patron of a charity dedicated to helping people maimed in this way to rebuild their lives. Find out about the work of such charities and their aims for people disabled by landmines.

Focus on: myth

RESEARCH . . .

— Aurelio fears that Parlanchina will 'marry a god', that is die before she marries, because she is so beautiful and charming that a god will want to carry her away for himself. Look up legends and fairy stories that tell what happens in relations between gods or spirits and mortals. You might read a dictionary of classical mythology for the story of Europa, or Psyche, or Daphne. Or you might read the European legends of Ondine or the Fisherman and the Seal. What do these stories suggest about the archetypes that have grown up in traditional accounts of human beings' relationships with the spirit world?

CHAPTERS 15 AND 16
(pp. 116–33)

Focus on: the theme of responsibility

ASK YOURSELF . . .
— Read the account of General Fuerte's 'trial' in Chapter 15. Remedios's gang find him 'sort-of-guilty' and 'sort-of-not-guilty' (p. 124). Bearing in mind the arguments put by Franco for the prosecution and by Garcia for the defence, what do you think? Is the General guilty or not guilty?

DISTINGUISH AND EVALUATE . . .
— Dona Constanza leads a life of ease. Is she guilty or not guilty of 'crimes against civilisation'?

Focus on: point of view

ACCOUNT FOR, RESEARCH AND RETELL . . .
— Rafael, Tomas and Gonzago look at Dona Constanza's old copy of *Vogue*. Read their reactions on p. 129. What do they see? What do you imagine the pictures look like? Even if you don't buy glossy magazines you will probably be able to guess. What does that suggest about the prevalence of marketing and the commercial presentation of women's bodies? Read Naomi Wolf's *The Beauty Myth* (Vintage, London, 1991) on the beauty industry and its influence. Is it possible to compare the propaganda of commerce in the beauty industry with the political propaganda of the various factions in *Don Emmanuel*?

CHAPTER 17
(pp. 134–41)

Focus on: point of view

ANALYSE . . .

— A new voice is introduced here speaking in the first person in the form of a letter. What is the impact of de Bernières using this different form of narration at this point in the story? And, given that we are now offered a perspective on Latin America from the point of view of a European settler, how does this letter throw light on the events and scenes that we have already encountered?

COMPARE AND CONTRAST . . .

— Look back at the end of Chapter 16 and Hugh Evans's return home. How does his point of view there compare with Antoine's in this chapter?

CHAPTERS 18, 19 AND 20
(pp. 142–66)

Focus on: plotting

ILLUSTRATE AND INTERPRET . . .

— Remedios plots, Don Emmanuel plots, Aurelio plots. Write out the plans of each one of them. What methods do they use to achieve their desired outcomes? What is each of them trying to do? In what ways are their methods and their motives similar?

EVALUATE . . .

— What role is Aurelio beginning to play in the novel as a whole? Remember what we have learned of his childhood and youth, and that he is an old man by the time he encounters Remedios.

Focus on: language and vocabulary

COMMENT ON . . .

— '"Are you a spy?" "I do not know the word," replied Aurelio. "I have eyes"' (p. 160). What does this exchange suggest about pejorative terms and the language that we use? Find other examples of exchanges in the novel as a whole where words are used, and misused, to convey a derogatory attitude.

CHAPTERS 21, 22, 23 AND 24
(pp. 167–208)

Focus on: plotting and the theme of values

LIST AND ILLUSTRATE . . .

— Dona Constanza falls for Gonzago and joins Remedios's gang. Felicidad is paid by Don Emmanuel to infect Figueras's men, and she gets paid by the men. Constanza and Gloria hatch a plot to get money out of Hugh and Remedios agrees to it. This group of chapters ends with Parlanchina. How far are other values beginning to be set against the anarchy of brutality and violence that has dominated the story so far? What do stories of the humiliation of Figueras (pp. 183–7) and the resistance of the radical lawyer (pp. 193–5) contribute to this change of tone?

CHAPTER 25
(pp. 209–17)

Focus on: myth and fairy stories

RESEARCH AND COMPARE . . .

— Read Marina Warner's *From the Beast to the Blonde: On Fairy Tales and their Tellers* (Vintage, London, 1995), or her *No Go the Bogeyman: Scaring, Lulling and Making Mock* (Vintage, London, 1998). Or else read Diane Purkiss's *Troublesome Things: A History of Fairies and Fairy Stories* (Allen Lane, London, 2000).

— Find stories which compare with what happens to Federico and Parlanchina. How has de Bernières adapted fairy stories to tell his new story?

Focus on: plotting

RELATE . . .

— Consider how the story of Federico and Parlanchina — while still the tale of a premature and violent death — might be read as a positive story, paralleling the stories of the women characters in the novel and their new control over events.

CHAPTER 26
(pp. 218–26)

Focus on: irony

STATE . . .

— Compare the title of this chapter with its contents. Why is it ironic?

CHAPTER 27
(pp. 227–34)

Focus on: narrative point of view

COMPARE . . .

— Look back at Antoine's other letter at pp. 134–41. How do the two compare? How has Antoine's objective 'European' view changed? What other information are we given here which might colour our view of other characters in the novel when looked at from Antoine's perspective?

CHAPTERS 28, 29 AND 30
(pp. 235–60)

Focus on: the theme of contrasts

DEFINE . . .

— Assess the subject matter and the tone of each of these three chapters. The first deals with a wedding – it includes a scene of a kind of battle and 'the girls win'. The second tells the story of Regina. The third takes us back to the more positive scene of the wedding with the return of Maria and the birth of her offspring. How do these contrasts work when set against one another by these narrative sequences?

Focus on: the theme of civil war

DISCUSS . . .

— On p. 260, Tomas says to Remedios, 'we have all killed our brothers today'. Discuss this statement in the light of the novel as a whole.

CHAPTER 31
(pp. 261–70)

Focus on: irony

ILLUSTRATE . . .
— What do the respective 'efforts' of these three men consist of? What is the literary effect of the various reports set out on pp. 262–4?

Focus on: the theme of history

RESEARCH . . .
— The President's military campaign described on pp. 267–70 is a parody of the events of the Falklands War that took place between Britain and Argentina in 1982. Find out what you can about the Falklands War and compare de Bernières's farcical fictional account with the events of that time.
— There is a mention of 'missing persons' on p. 265. During the years of the rule of the Argentine junta and during the repressive regimes of other South American countries many people did indeed disappear. An informal group grew up called 'The Mothers of the Disappeared'. Research this movement and compare their experiences and endeavours with those portrayed in de Bernières's novel as a whole.

CHAPTERS 32, 33 AND 34
(pp. 271–96)

Focus on: reference and allusion

RESEARCH . . .
— Read the Book of Exodus in the Old Testament of the Bible.

What comparisons can you draw between the events that led up to the exodus of the children of Israel out of Egypt and the motley group led by Remedios? Remember the stories of the plague of laughter and the plague of cats. Look carefully at what happens in this chapter and draw parallels. You should also look ahead to p. 333 at which point the travellers arrive where they will settle. Aurelio and Don Emmanuel appear there – who might they parallel among characters drawn from the biblical story?

Focus on: the theme of moral responsibility

COMPARE . . .

— Chapter 33 begins: 'It sometimes happens that in relatively powerless and impoverished countries there arise men of enormous vision who are frustrated and offended by the limitations of their lives, and seek to reach out for the stars on behalf of themselves and their nations' (p. 279). How does this statement relate to the stories of a) Badajoz and Buenanoce, and b) General Fuerte?

CHAPTERS 35, 36 AND 37
(pp. 297–321)

Focus on: the themes of revenge and redemption

CRITICALLY EVALUATE . . .

— The President starts to lose large sections of his army through 'accidents', and resorts to private pleasure. Set against the cynicism of this chapter is the increasing emphasis on the spiritual guiding that is taking the refugees in their 'biblical procession' up into the mountains, and the final elimination of Asado and his brigade of torturers. Consider your responses to each of these chapters and assess how the reactions of the reader are manipulated by choice of vocabulary, and by irony and satire.

RESEARCH . . .
— Look up 'Nemesis' in a dictionary of classical mythology. Strictly speaking, what does it mean? How is it relevant to Asado's fate?

CHAPTERS 38, 39 AND 40
(pp. 322–51)

Focus on: fact, fiction and the fantastic

DEFINE AND ANALYSE . . .
— Throughout *Don Emmanuel* de Bernières uses facts – like the phenomenon of 'the disappeared' and the Falklands War. However, the book is largely fiction, stories made up about places and characters that do not exist. And then many events in this novel are clearly fiction, but they are also fantastic – that is a fantasy – something that could never happen. Define which events come under which of these three headings in these chapters and in the novel as a whole. Look up the literary definition sometimes called 'magic realism'. Might this be an appropriate term for this novel?

CHAPTERS 41, 42 AND 43
(pp. 352–76)

Focus on: beginnings and endings

ASSESS AND OUTLINE . . .
— How many things begin in these chapters? How many end?

RESEARCH AND COMPARE . . .
— de Bernières's novel *Captain Corelli's Mandolin* ends with a

vision of three young girls. He discusses that ending in the interview included in this book. How does the ending to *Captain Corelli* compare with the ending to *Don Emmanuel*? It what ways is it the same? In what ways is it different?

Looking over the whole novel

QUESTIONS FOR ESSAYS OR DISCUSSION

1. 'Life is nothing if not a random motion of coincidences and quirks of chance; it never goes as planned or as foretold; frequently one gains happiness from being obliged to follow an unchosen path, or misery from following a chosen one' (p. 64). Discuss, in relation to events in *Don Emmanuel*.

2. Analyse the techniques and the forms of storytelling found in *Don Emmanuel*.

3. How does de Bernières create his imaginary Latin-American country?

4. 'de Bernières's worlds are fantastically real.' Discuss.

Señor Vivo and the Coca Lord

IN CLOSE-UP

Reading guides

SEÑOR VIVO AND THE COCA LORD

BEFORE YOU BEGIN TO READ . . .
Look at the interview with de Bernières and read the section on the Latin-American trilogy. You will see there that he identifies a number of themes including

- Political corruption
- Moral responsibility
- The presentation of character
- Writing about violence
- Magic
- The treatment of history

THE EPIGRAPH
The epigraph is a quotation from The Song of Songs, attributed to Solomon, from the Bible. Read it through, jot down some notes on what you think it means and what kinds of scenes it conjures up for you. When you have read the whole novel, look back at this epigraph and consider how it might relate to the story you have read.

PART I

PART I, CHAPTERS I–II
(pp. 3–43)

Focus on: storytelling

DISTINGUISH AND ASSESS . . .

— This novel is the second part of de Bernières's South American trilogy, so the narrative has to pick up the story here and remind us of what has gone before. The first words of the novel are 'Ever since . . .' referring back to episodes that we encountered in *The War of Don Emmanuel's Nether Parts*. Similarly on p. 9 Dionisio and Ramon have a conversation about how it is bad luck to shoot vultures – a superstition that was discussed in the first chapter of *Don Emmanuel*. Look for other such connective phrases and consider the narrative methods that recall and remind.

Focus on: tone

ANALYSE THE VOCABULARY . . .

— Read Chapter 2 on pp. 9–11. The facts of the scene that is being described here are brutal and violent. But the point is that this is an ordinary day and an ordinary occurrence in Dionisio's life. Write down the words that contribute to the tone that represents the banal. Is the shock element in this chapter made more forceful by the everyday tone of language? Look both at the language used by Ramon and Dionisio, and that used by the narrator.

— Look at the title of Chapter 7, 'Dionisio is Given a Hand'. Is this funny? How would you describe the tone adopted here? Is it ironic, cruel, amusing, cynical?

CONSIDER . . .
— Chapter 2 begins with Dionisio getting out of bed in the morning. So do Chapters 7 and 13. True, in real life, that's what we do. But this is fiction, so why do you think so many of the chapters begin this way?

Focus on: literary form

SEARCH AND ASSESS . . .
— On p. 3 we are told that the President has taken to reading *La Prensa* and especially the letters of Dionisio Vivo about the coca trade. Dionisio's crusade against the drug dealers will be the main focus of this story, but his letters – and those of others – will create a literary pattern that shapes the story. Look at the chapters in the section that are in the form of letters (Chapters 3, 5, 6 and 10) and assess the different styles that are used by each character. What literary effect is achieved by the use of letters? How important is it that we hear the voices of the characters without the mediation of the narrator?

Focus on: allusion and characterisation

RESEARCH . . .
— Dionisio's name is a version of the Greek name Dionysius. Look up Dionysius in a dictionary of classical mythology. As you begin to build up a picture of his character, consider why it might be that he has been given this name? And what is the relevance of his second name 'Vivo'? In Chapter 7 Ramon calls Dionisio 'Empedocles'. He explains why on p. 24. On p. 22 Ramon calls him 'Diogenes'. Look that name up in a dictionary of classical mythology. How do these allusions contribute to Dionisio's characterisation?

Focus on: words and meaning

CONSIDER . . .
— On p. 28 the narrator considers how the meaning of words can change or be revised. How does this reflection relate to the themes of the novel as a whole?

PART I, CHAPTERS 12–23
(pp. 44–100)

Focus on: literary style and the theme of contrasts

COMPARE . . .
— Read the four chapters entitled 'The Grand Candomble of Cochadebajo de los Gatos'. If you have read the first part of the trilogy you will know all these characters. The events described here are mystical and bizarre. Sometimes they involve magic, often they are rumbustious and funny.
— Then read Dionisio's letter in Chapter 13 (pp. 48–51). The third person narrative of the four connected chapters is light-hearted, ironic and broadly comic. Dionisio's letter is a piece of rhetoric designed to persuade and reform. What is the effect of the contrasts set up between the carefree life of the inhabitants of Cochadebajo de los Gatos, and the harsher scenes in the world of the drug dealers and their victims?

Focus on: plot

WORK OUT THE PATTERN . . .
— Dionisio keeps getting warnings about his active resistance to the coca lords and his public crusade. And yet he ignores them, or misses the point altogether. Or else, the plots fail, by sheer accident of fate (as with the bomb on p. 78),

and therefore he never gets to realise the danger he is in. Dionisio and Anica go on with their lives blissfully unaware. But we – the readers – might guess that the threat is real. Trace the ways in which the irony of his ignorance is made into a device for driving the story on.

ASK YOURSELF . . .

— When you get to Chapter 21 consider the reversal of expectation that we undergo in discovering that it was Ramon who had 'captured' Dionisio. Ask yourself if you think Ramon's actions are justified. When you have read to the end of the novel, ask yourself the same question.

Focus on: voice

CONSIDER . . .

— Chapter 19 begins with a speech by an unknown person. Analyse the presentation of the voice here. What kind of character is this speaking? How seriously should we take this? What is the effect of having the speech in inverted commas, but not attributed so that we can make no deductions about character except from the language used and what is said.

Focus on: allusion

RESEARCH . . .

— Ramon again calls Dionisio many names on p. 66, and on pp. 84–5. Look up these names. Who were these characters in history and legend? How do they relate to the story and the character of Dionisio?

PART 1, CHAPTERS 24–34
(pp. 101–157)

Focus on: voice and characterisation

EVALUATE . . .

— Consider what you know about Anica by now. What does it add to hear her own voice here in this first entry from her journal? Why do you imagine that her voice is introduced now? When you have finished reading to the end of the novel, ask yourself that question again.

DESCRIBE AND ASSESS . . .

— Look at the description of some of the minor characters in this section: Leticia Aragon (pp. 115–18), La Prima Primavera (p. 143 on), the Naked Admiral (p. 145 on) or Fulgencia Astiz (p. 125 on). Make a note of their key characteristics. How far would you consider these to be fully developed characters? Or is their significance metaphoric or symbolic? If so, how do they relate to the main action of the story, and in what ways does their introduction serve to mirror or counterpoint the main story?

Focus on: allusion

RESEARCH . . .

— Look up the 'Maenads' and the 'Bacchantes' (p. 130) in a dictionary of classical mythology. How might the stories that you will find there reflect on the events that are unfolding in this novel?

Focus on: plot and patterning

LOOK FOR . . .

— We learn that the women pursuing Dionisio are nicknamed

148

'Las Locas' . . . 'the mad women'. The final words of the novel are '"You are all locos," he said.' Look for as many references of this kind as you can. How do they pattern the plot of the novel? Who do you think is mad? And why?

PART II

THE EPIGRAPH
Read the epigraph and compare it with that which preceded Part I. When you have read to the end of the novel, consider how each of the epigraphs relates to the action of the story.

PART II, CHAPTERS 35–43
(pp. 159–193)

Focus on: characterisation and plot

CRITICALLY EVALUATE . . .
— This section begins with Anica's voice. And, increasingly, the focus of the narrative is on Anica's story and her point of view. Consider why this might be – you will have to ask yourself the question again when you have finished reading the novel. Evaluate this shift at the centre of the novel away from Dionisio and towards Anica.

CONTRAST AND COMPARE . . .
— This section also offers more of the story of Lazaro. How might his story parallel or relate to Anica's?

PART II, CHAPTERS 44–55
(pp. 194–259)

Focus on: language, meaning and misunderstanding

EXPLAIN . . .

— Chapter 48 is called 'Anica's Last Mistake'. What is her mistake? The failure to express herself and make herself clear to Dionisio (p. 224)? Or might it be something else? Do you think she has made the right choice?

Focus on: plot

JUSTIFY . . .

— From Chapter 48 on, it is Dionisio's point of view that once more dominates. Obviously this is partly because Anica has left him, but what other reasons might there be in terms of the working out of the idea of heroism and resistance to corruption?

Focus on: irony

COMMENT ON . . .

— de Bernières speaks about Chapter 49 in the interview. Consider the irony in the title to this chapter, 'Another Statistic'.
— On p. 253 we learn that it was Anica's father who sent the thugs to scare her into leaving Dionisio, so that she was no longer as safe as she would have been with him while the superstitions accrued around him. And yet on p. 254 Dionisio recognises that Anica died because of his crusade. Who do you think is responsible for Anica's death?

Focus on: the theme of heroism in the everyday

ASSESS . . .

— Chapter 55 begins with Dionisio getting out of bed again.

Look back at the earlier chapters that began in this way and compare those episodes with this. Now Dionisio has lost his lover and his friend to his crusade. Is that qualitatively different from the unknown victims who were used at the beginning to make the coca lord's point? Consider particularly the narrative tone in the earlier chapters as against the narrative tone of this penultimate chapter.

PART III

PART III, CHAPTER 56 AND EPILOGUE
(pp. 263–280)

Focus on: voice, perspective and point of view

DEFINE AND EXPLAIN . . .
— In Chapter 56 a new character is introduced to assess Dionisio's work and his fame as a hero. What new perspectives on the story are raised with this alteration in the narrative viewpoint? How reliable is this narrator?

Focus on: the theme of corruption

EXPLAIN . . .
— Explain the significance of the Epilogue.

Looking over the whole novel

QUESTIONS FOR ESSAYS OR DISCUSSION
1. How convinced are you by the characterisation of Dionisio Vivo?

2. Is the portrayal of explicit violence in this novel justified?

3. Consider how the real and the magical jostle against one another in *Señor Vivo*. How effective is this literary technique?

4. 'Anica is the most important character in *Señor Vivo and the Coca Lord*'. Discuss.

5. Analyse the ways in which de Bernières plays with language in this novel.

The Troublesome Offspring of Cardinal Guzman

IN CLOSE-UP

Reading guides

THE TROUBLESOME OFFSPRING OF CARDINAL GUZMAN

BEFORE YOU BEGIN TO READ . . .
Look at the interview with de Bernières and read the section on the Latin-American trilogy. You will see there that de Bernières identifies a number of themes including

- Political corruption
- Moral responsibility
- The presentation of character
- Writing about violence
- Magic
- The treatment of history

Other themes might include:

- Storytelling
- Men and women

While you are reading in detail it is worth bearing these overall themes in mind.

PART I

PROLOGUE
(pp. 1–2)

PART I: CHAPTERS 1–6
(pp. 5–38)

Focus on: addresser, address, addressee

EXAMINE . . .

— Look at each of these seven sections; that is, the Prologue and the first six chapters. Write down who does the telling or narrating, what kind of 'address' they are making — is it a speech, personal confession, a third-person account? — and then write the name or names, or the identity of the audience to whom each section is addressed. How many different kinds of addresser are in here, and address, and addressee?

Focus on: genre and style

ANALYSE . . .

— From your reading of these opening chapters, how would you define the genre and the style that de Bernières is using in *The Troublesome Offspring of Cardinal Guzman*? Choose from: exemplum, fable, fantastic literature, satire, parable, pastiche, parody, picaresque, pastoral, comedy, tragedy, travesty and burlesque. Look these terms up in a dictionary of literary terms. Which might most closely approximate to which chapter(s)?

Focus on: allusion and reference

COMPARE AND CONTRAST . . .

— In Chapter 2, the Mexican musicologist has composed a famous arrangement on a (borrowed) tune. In Chapter 3, Dona

Constanza is opening a new restaurant. If you have read de Bernières's *Captain Corelli's Mandolin* then you will know that music and food are important there too. Make a comparison between the ways in which the two texts exploit these themes.

RESEARCH . . .
— When the new priest arrives he quotes Latin; however, it is not Church Latin but scurrilious poems by the Roman poet Gaius Valerius Catullus (*c.* 84–*c.* 54 BC). Find out about Catullus and read translations of some of his poems. How do they help to bring out the themes of the novel as a whole?

RESEARCH AND COMPARE . . .
— Lena and Ena play a 'bed trick' on the Mexican musicologist. It is a common plot device in a number of Renaissance plays, as is the confusion that arises when twins – not necessarily identical twins – are repeatedly mistaken for each other. Look up a 'bed trick' play. This might be Shakespeare's *Measure for Measure* or Middleton and Rowley's *The Changeling*. For twin plays, look at Shakespeare's *Twelfth Night* or *The Comedy of Errors*. What issues to do with identity and the perception of individuality are raised in those plays and in de Bernières's novel as a whole?

Focus on: the theme of public and private

RESEARCH AND CRITICALLY EVALUATE . . .
— Read Naomi Klein's account of globalisation in *No Logo* (Flamingo, London, 2000). *Cardinal Guzman* begins with a reference in the Prologue to the global power of 'the most powerful soft-drinks company in the world'. It then offers the perspective of Cardinal Guzman who is part of the worldwide enterprise of the Catholic Church. In these early chapters of the novel, consider how large public and commercial

endeavours are set against private experience and personal morality. Can you find other examples in these chapters? (What happens to the tune composed by the Mexican musicologist, for instance?)

PART I, CHAPTERS 7–12
(pp. 39–81)

Focus on: parallels and point of view

EXPLAIN . . .

— This series of chapters alternates between three 'submissions' of the Holy Office addressed to His Eminence, and the personal stories – told in the third and in the first persons – about the settlement at Cochadebajo de los Gatos. How do the themes and the points of view revealed and displayed in each reinforce – or contradict – the themes and points of view in the others?

Focus on: vocabulary

LOOK UP . . .

— On p. 52, the narrative describes the crowd that turns out to see the windlass devised by Profesor Luis and built by the people as a 'pharaonic' spectacle. Look up this word in a dictionary. What does it mean? To what does it refer? If you read the interview with Louis de Bernières included in this book, you will see that he describes how words interest him, and how he even tries to make up words. On p. 53, the mayor makes a speech in praise of Profesor Luis that includes the words: behemoth, leviathan, juggernaut and mammoth. Look up these words too. Note down the derivation of each. What do they mean? And from what languages and cultures are they borrowed?

— There are many words in the English language which are neologisms — new words or phrases. They are usually derived in five ways: through borrowing (taken from another language), compounding (joining two words), through acronym (based on the initial letters or syllables of other words), blending (merging two or more words together), or clipping (abbreviating a word). Note down cases where you spot such words as you read. Which kinds of characters are more likely to use which kind of neologism?

PART I, CHAPTERS 13–19
(pp. 82–117)

Focus on: characterisation

ILLUSTRATE AND DEFINE . . .
— Look over all of these chapters. The Cardinal appears several times, but in different incarnations — in his relation with Don Susto, in his relation with his mistress Concepion, and in his relation with the President. What kind of picture of his character are you beginning to build up? Define his character in relation to each of these three important persons in his life. For each of the three, write three sentences describing the Cardinal as he is perceived from their point of view. Now write three sentences describing the Cardinal's character from the point of view of the child Cristobal.

RESEARCH AND COMPARE . . .
— Read the 'Prologue to the Wife of Bath's Tale' in Geoffrey Chaucer's *The Canterbury Tales* (c. 1387). You might also like to read her Tale about the 'loathly lady'. Then look at Chapters 14 and 15 of *Cardinal Guzman*. Compare the attitudes and opinions of the Wife of Bath with those of Remedios and Concepion.

Focus on: characterisation and the theme of moral responsibility

INTERPRET . . .

— On p. 94, the narrative tells us that the Cardinal 'began to rely upon his office rather than his humanity in order to get things done'. Discuss the relevance of this remark in relation to the various characters in the novel and in relation to the themes of the novel as a whole.

PART I, CHAPTERS 20–27
(pp. 118–62)

Focus on: the theme of storytelling

TRACE . . .

— There are several different, but related, stories about stories in this section. Write down as many as you can find. These might include: the plague of reading, as everyone wants to read *Dona Barbara*; the story that the Cardinal tells Cristobal about the Passion of Christ; the list of books that are burned in Rincondondo; Fuerte's account of Aurelio's stories (p. 135); and the story of Fuerte's youthful passion for a redhead. How many others can you find? Contrast and compare the relevance of these stories to the novel as a whole.

RESEARCH AND COMPARE . . .

— Read Jeanette Winterson's short story 'Turn of the World' in *The World and Other Places* (Vintage, London, 1999), pp. 149–60. It is partly a story about storytelling. Compare that story with the stories about stories in de Bernières's novel. What qualities are similar? What makes each or some of the stories sound like fairy tales? Consider language, sentence structures, characterisation and plot in each case.

DISCUSS . . .

— 'Fiction is not about anything real, and shall not be fought over' (p. 122). Consider this statement in relation to a) de Bernières's novels – you might like to look at the interview to get some more information on this – and b) what you know of the world's attitudes to books and stories.

Focus on: jokes

EXPLAIN . . .

— The General suffers from the effects of the torture he has previously endured. On p. 158, we are told that he 'tried hard not to breathe too deeply, and attempted to avoid gesticulation as he talked; he was beginning to feel like an Englishman'. What is the joke? Is it funny? Look for literary terms that describe this mixture of the horrific and the amusing, the sad and the absurd.

PART I, CHAPTERS 28–34
(pp. 163–208)

Focus on: the theme of history

DISTINGUISH AND CRITICALLY EVALUATE . . .

— This section begins with an argument about history. 'There has been much argument amongst historiosophists as to what conditions must pertain in order for history to occur' (p. 163). Consider the absurdity of this statement. Read the paragraphs that follow it and then look over the section for other discussion of what history is and how it is used. Look also at the interview with de Bernières where he discusses his own distrust of official 'history' and why he feels like that. How is this theme played out in the novel as a whole?

Focus on: the theme of music

TRACE AND COMPARE . . .
— The Mexican musicologist came to the settlement at Cochadebajo de los Gatos because of a piece of music. Now Concepion gives the Cardinal a present of a record of Beethoven's *Eroica* symphony. Compare the portrayals of each of these two pieces of music in this section.

PART TWO

PART II, CHAPTERS 35–43
(pp. 211–55)

Focus on: the theme of storytelling

ASSESS AND CRITICALLY EVALUATE . . .
'"It appears that we have a wonderful specimen of a growth that has been burgeoning inside you since the day of your nativity. It consists of a randomly assembled chaos of normal bodily components that have proliferated in an unstructured manner from a totipotential germ"' (pp. 227–8). This is the doctor's description of the 'monster' growing inside the Cardinal. In the 1831 preface to her novel, Mary Shelley described *Frankenstein* (1819) – which is about the making of a creature without the natural methods of procreation – as 'my hideous progeny'. Henry James famously described the nineteenth-century novel as a 'loose baggy monster'.
— Read all the descriptions of the Cardinal's living monster. Consider how far the 'monster' may resemble the methods and technique of de Bernières's novel as a whole. In what ways does the description of the Cardinal's monster exactly mirror the literary patterns and styles of the novel itself?

RESEARCH AND COMPARE . . .

— Look for stories in legend and myth where human beings turn into birds, or where their souls are thought to return in the shape of birds. Compare the episode with the humming-bird (pp. 248–9) with the stories you can find.

PART II, CHAPTERS 44–49
(pp. 256–90)

Focus on: patriotism and its discontents

OUTLINE AND RETELL . . .

— During Don Emmanuel's 'patriotic concert' in Chapter 45 he succeeds in offending the British Ambassador. How does he do this? What do you think of his techniques?

— Consider these key words: patriotism, nationalism, respect, difference, multiplicity, diversity, pride. Write down definitions for each of them. Then imagine each word positively. Write down the definition again. Then imagine each word negatively and write down the definition again. Which deliberately posi-tive or negative definitions most closely approximated to the definitions you had originally written down? What does this tell you about your own positions and attitudes? How do they relate to the events in the novel as a whole?

Focus on: voice and point of view

ACCOUNT FOR . . .

— We hear Aurelio's own voice here, although his words are written down by General Fuerte. How important is it that this comes at this point in the trilogy, given that we have followed Aurelio from the beginning? What values – overall – do Aurelio's voice and presence in the novels represent?

163

ASSESS . . .

— Concepion tells the Cardinal a proverb: 'Why does God let babies die? Go and ask the butterflies, because they don't know any better than anyone else' (p. 278). Why might it be important that it is Concepion who tells this to the Cardinal? Remember their respective social status. How might the implications of this proverb relate to the events played out in the novel as a whole?

INTERPRET . . .

— Aurelio tells Parlanchina a joke. 'Once there was a woman worm who met her friend under the floor of my hut, and I heard them talking. One said to the other, "Where is your husband?" and the other replied, "He has gone fishing"' (p. 289). How does the serious side of this joke relate to the themes of voice and point of view, men and women, and political irony as they are worked out in the novel as a whole?

PART II, CHAPTERS 50–55
(pp. 291–323)

Focus on: allusion and reference

RESEARCH . . .

— At the beginning of Chapter 50, Sibila is introduced through a dream about ancient Greece (p. 291). Look up the stories about the Sibyl in a dictionary of classical mythology. How do those stories compare with the ways in which Sibila is presented in *Cardinal Guzman*?

— 'Parlanchina's Lament', in Chapter 51, is a virtuoso performance taking us back through her stories and her losses across the whole trilogy. Look up the 'Song of Songs' in the Old Testament of the Bible. In what ways are the language and the imagery and the structure of this lament similar to the biblical model? In what ways are they different?

— The chapters that deal with Sibila and her martyrdom are – to some extent – based on the terrors of the Inquisition, a notorious religious regime, endorsed and denied at various times by the Catholic Church, that had pledged itself to purge heretics and assert the predominance of the true faith. Many suffered under its violent sway, and the grand auto-da-fé, as practised in Spain during the fifteenth and sixteenth centuries, was the centrepiece of their reign of terror. On the occasion of an auto-da-fé – the judicial sentence of 'act of [the] faith' ordered by the Inquisition – heretics would be taken to a public place to be burned.

— Read Sara Maitland's 'The Burning Times' (1984). This is a story set in the Middle Ages, about a woman who is burned as a witch. The story is told from the point of view of her daughter, and, though the daughter is the one who has betrayed her, the mother – like Sibila – forgives the child even in the moment of her suffering. Compare this story to this episode in *The Troublesome Offspring of Cardinal Guzman*.

PART II, CHAPTERS 56–63
(pp. 324–67)

Focus on: narrative and point of view

COMPARE . . .

— Each one of these letters in Chapter 56 is composed by different characters whom we have met in the course of reading the trilogy and each letter ties up a particular aspect of the plot. Consider the different voices that we hear in this section. In what ways might this chapter constitute a summary of the whole of the novel – and the trilogy as a whole?

PART II, CHAPTERS 64–65
(pp. 368–79)

Focus on: endings

LOOK BACK AND SUMMARISE . . .

— Many of the events that take place in these last two chapters are like events, or replay and revise events, that we have seen before in the trilogy. Identify as many of these as you can and summarise the conclusions to the story, both in literal terms, with regard to the plot, and in metaphoric terms, with regard to images and metaphors.

Focus on: literary forms

DEFINE . . .

— On p. 376, Dionisio says: 'Quite an epic . . .' In what ways is the word 'epic' a summary of the trilogy as a whole. Look up 'epic' in a dictionary of literary terms.

PART II, EPILOGUE
(pp. 380–8)

ASSESS YOUR OWN KNOWLEDGE . . .

— The Epilogue provides conclusions to various stories. Often we are not given the names of the characters that the short sections relate to. All the same, how many of them do you know? Consider how your own memory of the three books in the trilogy and the characters therein is enough to enable you to recognise each individual style of speech or their particular personal predicament.

COMPARE AND CONTRAST . . .

— Look at the last line of *Cardinal Guzman* on p. 388. Where have you heard something similar before? Look back at *Don Emmanuel* if you cannot think of the answer – p. 1, to be precise. Why do you suppose that de Bernières has chosen to end the trilogy in this way? Is it just a neat literary device? Might there be more to it?

Looking over the whole novel

QUESTIONS FOR ESSAYS OR DISCUSSION

1. Read the dedication, and the epigraph to Part 1 that appears on p. 3. How do they relate to the novel as a whole?

2. Read the epigraph to Part 2 on p. 209. How might it relate to the themes of the novel as a whole?

3. What is the significance of de Bernières's use of lengthy chapter headings?

4. Analyse the role music plays in the novel.

5. *The Troublesome Offspring of Cardinal Guzman* has been described as 'farcical'. Would you agree?

6. Discuss the importance of the idealised community of Cochadebajo de los Gatos in relation to the novel as a whole.

7. 'de Bernières's Latin American trilogy is a meditation on "machismo".' Do you agree?

Contexts, Comparisons, and Complementary Readings

THE WAR OF DON EMMANUEL'S NETHER PARTS

SEÑOR VIVO AND THE COCA LORD

THE TROUBLESOME OFFSPRING OF CARDINAL GUZMAN

Focus on: literary style

RESEARCH AND COMPARE . . .
De Bernières's South American trilogy is set in an imaginary
Latin American country that is based on his own experience
of living in Columbia. He discusses this in the interview. He
uses a mixture of 'realist' writing, where minute physical details
and circumstantial descriptions of places and characters are
included, with 'magic' events, such as the miracles of the cats,
the plagues in *Don Emmanuel* or the mysterious bringing back
to life of Aurelio. Look up the term 'realist' in a glossary of
literary terms and look up 'magic realism' too. Other books
that are classed under the heading of 'magic realism' might

include Gabriel Garcia Marquez's *One Hundred Years of Solitude*, Angela Carter's *The Magic Toyshop* or *Nights at the Circus*, Isabel Allende's *The House of the Spirits* and Ben Okri's *Songs of Enchantment* or *The Famished Road*.

Read any of these books and compare their versions of 'magic realism' with that employed by de Bernières.

Focus on: South America and the theme of the treatment of history

RESEARCH . . .
Though the trilogy is set in an imaginary Latin American country, many of the scenes and events described – whether the corruption of the police, the drug dealing, the poverty, the disappearances, or the routine use of torture by the State – are derived from the facts of history under the various totalitarian regimes that ruled in states such as Chile, Argentina or Brazil in the late twentieth century. Find out about such regimes and consider how de Bernières has adapted the facts into fiction.

Focus on: the presentation of torture

RESEARCH AND CONSIDER . . .
While the civilised world broadly agrees today that the use of torture is a contravention of human rights, there are statistics which reveal that it is as common today as it ever was and as ingenious. Amnesty International is committed to seeking out and shaming those states that use torture as a means of political control over its citizens or its enemies. Contact them at 99 Rosebery Avenue, London ECIR 4RE if you would like to know more about their campaigns. In Britain the Medical Foundation for Victims of Torture founded by Helen Bamber

provides practical support for many people who are refugees from such regimes. Contact them at Star House, 104–8 Grafton Road, London NW5 4BD if you would like to help or know more about their work.

COMPARE . . .

De Bernières talks about writing about violence in the interview. It is a hard thing to do and some readers object to this aspect of his work. Read the following extract from Helen Gordon Liddle's *The Prisoner: A Sketch (An Experience of Forcible Feeding)* by a Suffragette (Garden City Press Ltd., Letchworth, 1911). It is from a firsthand account of force feeding. Helen Gordon Liddle was a follower of Emmeline Pankhurst who campaigned for votes for women. The Suffragettes protested in public places and were often arrested for breach of the peace. In prison they would go on hunger strike to draw attention to their cause, and that is why many of them were force fed.

Consider the kinds of language Helen Gordon Liddle uses to describe her actual experience of violence, and compare it with the style and methods used in his fiction by de Bernières.

The prisoner is at her weakest this morning – her physical powers are at their lowest ebb – her mouth, which has been so tortured, is ulcerated, and shrinking from the slightest touch.

In his right hand the man holds an instrument they call a gag, partly covered with indiarubber, which part the prisoner never feels, and the moment of battle has come.

The prisoner refuses to unclose her teeth – the last defence against the food she, out of principle, refuses to take – the doctor has his 'duty' to perform – his dignity also to maintain before five

women and a tall junior doctor. His temper is short
– has already been ruffled. So he sets about his job
in a butcherly fashion – there is no skill required for
this job – only brutality. He puts his great fingers
along her teeth – feels a gap at the back, rams the
tool blindly and with evident intention to hurt her,
and cause the helpless woman to wince – along the
shrinking flesh – how long will it take before superior strength triumphs? – tears start in the prisoner's
eyes – uncontrollable tears – tears she would give
anything to control.

It is still dark in the cell and the man strains at
her mouth blindly, without result. 'Can you see?'
asks the junior doctor. 'No,' blusters the other,
'better bring a light.' But he does not wait until the
taper is brought – ah – at last he has forced the tool
in, and with leverage the jaw opens.

He has still to hold it for twenty minutes or so
while the food is being poured or pushed or choked
down her throat – unluckily the gag has been forced
in so carelessly that it has caught in the cheek,
between it and the sharp teeth below.

The pain is maddening – she strains at her hands
– her feet are in a vice – her head is held – she tries
to speak – her jaw is forced to its widest. They pour
the food down – it is a mince of meat and brown
bread and milk – too dry – too stiff – they hold her
nose that she cannot breathe, and so she must
breathe with her mouth and swallow at the same
time, the doctors helping it in with hot hands that
have handled a pipe and heaven knows how many
patients – scraping their fingers clean on her teeth,
from the horrible mess.

It would seem they were not doctors, for they

force it down so heedlessly that the prisoner chokes and gasps for breath, the tears pouring from her eyes. The young doctor is called away – the pain is too much for her – she moves her head – the doctor gives another twist, and the nurse, to get it over sooner, pours the food quicker.

The limit is reached, and for the first time the prisoner gives way – great sobs of pain and breathlessness come faster and faster – she cannot bear it – she tries to call out 'Stop!' with that tortured wide-open mouth – and with one wrench she frees her hands and seizes the gag.

The doctor says to the officers – 'She says it is hot.' 'No,' they cry – the horror of the scene upon them – 'she said stop.'

A short quick thrust and her mouth is gagged again – the prisoner tries to control herself – her sobs increase – her breathlessness also – there is nothing but the pain and the relentless forcing of food down her throat – her choking despair, and the bitter draught of tonic and digestive medicine which is also poured down her throat.

At last it is over, and she is left sick and shaken with the whole scene. She sits up – tearing at the now filthy cloth surrounding her neck, and with a shudder of revolting disgust throws it from her. The officers, too, are silent – she who had dreaded it has left the cell at once, looking white as death – now another goes hurriedly away with white face – the prisoner is dressed – her bed is made, and the day begins – oh, how wretched she is.

VINTAGE
LIVING
TEXTS

Reference

Selected extracts from reviews

These brief extracts from contemporary reviews of de Bernières's work are designed to be used to suggest angles on the text that may be relevant to the themes of the books, or to their settings, to their literary methods, to their historical contexts, or to indicate their relevance to issues, questions or problems today.

Sometimes one reviewer's opinion will be entirely contradicted by another's. You might use these passages to ask yourself whether or not you agree with the writer's assessments. Or else you may take phrases from these reviews to use for framing questions – for discussion, or for essays – about the texts.

The excerpts here have been chosen because they offer useful and intelligent observations. In general, though, when you are reading reviews in newspapers, it is best to remember two things: they are often written under pressure, and they have to give the reader some idea of what the book under discussion is like, so they do tend to give space to summarising the plot.

None of these critical opinions are the last word. They are simply contributions to a cultural debate. As such, they should be approached with intellectual interest – because they can give the mood and tone of a particular time – and they should be treated with caution – because the very fact of that prevailing mood and time may intervene.

Cressida Connolly, 16th April 1994
From *The Spectator*
On the theme of history

Captain Corelli's Mandolin is set on the island of Cephallonia in Greece during and since the last war. Like many a British writer before him, de Bernières has clearly fallen under the spell of what he describes as 'the little nation that has given Europe its culture, its impetus, its heart'. He might also have said its gift for tragedy. The events chronicled here are as terrible and relentless as any ancient drama. The miracle is that he manages to introduce such humour into this dreadful saga.

I should confess that my knowledge of modern Greek history is not just slender, but anorexic. Reading here of British lethargy, of Italian and then German invasions followed by mayhem, slaughter and atrocity, I very much hoped that he was making it all up. Of course he is not: the central event of this novel is the actual murder of more than 4,000 Italian soldiers by the Germans in Cephallonia. De Bernières does not shirk from describing horror, as readers of his previous novels will remember. Rare among contemporary writers, though, his accounts of violence and brutality are never superfluous. He is old fashioned, too, in his values: carnage may be depicted explicitly, but love-scenes are touchingly chaste, with nobody going much further than kissing. He recognises honour and celebrates valour.

Andrew Post, April 1994
From the *Literary Review*
On the theme of history

The other constant theme is the influence of history, the way that our behaviour is shaped by the precedents of the past: Pelagia watching her fiancé swimming thinks that 'perhaps this same scene had been enacted generation after generation since Mycenean times; perhaps in the time of Odysseus there had been young girls like herself who had gone down to the sea in order to spy on the nakedness of those they loved'. Characters act as they do with an eye on the judgement of posterity: Mussolini is desperate for a war that will fortify his place in history, while the Greek dictator Metaxas, realising too late that, for all his friendship with the Axis powers, he is a poodle amongst wolves, earns his own place in history by resisting the Fascist ultimatum. Mandras believes that he can be made worthy of Pelagia by winning martial glory, and when that hope fades he transfers his affections to Communism, whose historical necessity justifies any amount of brutality and treachery.

For de Bernières, it is zealots who are the villains: his heroes are those, of whatever race, who have 'the moral authority of someone who refuses to compromise an ethical principle in the name of the ideal', and who allow friendship to survive the most extreme tests. These tests are extreme indeed. This version of the Second World War in Greece is not the sunny idyll of the film *Mediterraneo*; de Bernières writes with horrifying, graphic physicality of the suffering of war, of the effects of starvation and cold,

of atrocities and betrayals. When Italy joins the
Allies, the Germans turn on the Italian garrison on
the island, slaughtering their former friends, whilst
Britain and America do nothing to help. After
Liberation, Greece falls into a vicious and bitter civil
war, as Mandras and his fellow Communists try to
liberate the masses by torture, rape and theft.
'History repeats itself, first as tragedy and then again
as tragedy.'

A. S. Byatt, 25th April 1994
From *The Evening Standard*
On form, tone and style

This is a great rambling novel which accommodates
the first person musings of dictators, letters from
innumerable lovers, political pamphlets and diary sections within its capacious narrative. Characters –
such as Lulu, the distracting and promiscuous
daughter of Metaxas, the Greek dictator – make
brief appearances in cameo roles only to be aban-
doned without explanation.

Like Dickens, de Bernières gets away with heart-
warming, tear-jerking sentimentality, but counter-
balances sentiment with clinical observation of the
workings of violence, describing maggot-infested
rotting flesh on live bodies, or the agonising mal-
functioning of a starving man's gut. It is all the
more remarkable that with tragedy and bloody
destruction all around, he is able to sustain the
essentially comic tone.

David Horspool, 8th April 1994
From the *Times Literary Supplement*
On style and tone

De Bernières sees that war can either degrade or ele-
vate human beings, but it is humanity itself rather
than war's effects which interests him. The lightness
of the early chapters, when Iannis cures a long-deaf
patient by removing a dried pea from his ear, or
when Father Arsenios collapses drunk behind a holy
screen which only he is allowed to pass, never completely disappears. When a British agent parachutes
into Cephallonia, a goatherd mistakes him for an
angel, an impression reinforced by his speaking
incomprehensible ancient Greek (rendered by de
Bernières as Chaucerian English). Humour and
humanity make the chorus of voices telling de
Bernières's story not only comprehensible, but har-
monious to the ear.

Roz Kaveney, 22nd April 1994
From *The New Statesman and Society*
On the mix of styles in the Latin American trilogy
and in *Captain Corelli's Mandolin*

Some flavours go together by natural sympathy,
others work together as a tension. Louis de Bernières
has made a promising career out of novels in which
the sentimentally, whimsically sweet and the brutally,
realistically sour play off each other. This worked in
his three novels of Latin America, where satirical
portraits of illiterate, thuggish heads of state co-
existed with resurrected conquistadors and journeys

to secluded Utopias. His actual knowledge of the area whose literature, in its magical-realist incarnation, he was colonising so assiduously prevented this work from ever quite becoming cheap.

His flair for the sardonic takes nervy risks with good taste and with sneering capitalisation on others' problems, but it never teeters over the border. There is enough of his own artistic personality – sharp, sparky, tear-jerking – in the mix, that the world of these novels is not the *Hundred Years of Solitude* theme park that it can sound like in synopsis . . .

The horrors of war, revolution, massacre and earthquake are in any case the background to the doomed love affair between Corelli and Pelagia. De Bernières cheerfully ladles on to this every syrupy cliché of romance, down to the series of misunderstandings that keeps them apart until the end of the book. What is modern is the sense that the lives they have had apart were fulfilling even in their joint sense of loss: the work into which they threw themselves is at least as permanent as their love. If I have a reservation about this generally excellent novel, it is that a book capable of selling us such a tough-minded perception perhaps no longer needed all the apparatus of coincidence and omens and comic strong men. At times, the magic gets in the way of realism.

Glossary of Literary Terms

Anachronism When a literary reference is made to an object, event, person or thing that is completely out of place in the natural order in time. For example, in Shakespeare's 'Julius Caesar' a clock chimes although the play is set in Roman times, long before clocks were invented.

Authorial Voice The voice of the author.

Burlesque Broadly speaking this term refers to all types of satiric imitation. In particular when literature or theatre spoof other theatrical or literary genres with the intent of illuminating the folly of certain customs, people or institutions. The defining characteristic of burlesque is the discrepancy between its content and its style. *High Burlesque* employs a traditional style to discuss trivia. For example the 'rude mechanicals'' play in Shakespeare's *A Midsummer Nights Dream*. *Low Burlesque* mocks serious events or issues.

Caricature A ridiculous exaggeration of personal traits. For example a caricature of an actress would be someone who is melodramatic, insecure, and constantly wanting to perform.

Characterisation The way in which an author creates and then 'fleshes out' a character. Skilled fiction writers can create utterly believable characters through their choices of the characters' dress, speech and actions.

Clichés An expression that has been overused so much it has lost its original vivacity and clarity of expression. For example 'Sharp as a tack'. Any obvious or time-honoured plots, themes or characters are also considered clichéd. For example the cackling villain or the weeping heroine.

Comedy A literary work that seeks to amuse its audience. Usually this involves humorous situations featuring everyday characters employing ordinary language. There are however, many different forms of comedy, such as the Comedy of Manners that uses wit to ridicule social codes and pretensions of the day. For example the TV show 'Keeping up Appearances'. See also Burlesque, Satire and Pastiche.

Epic The traditional Epic form is a long narrative poem that conforms to certain literary conventions. Epic tales usually detail the exploits of a larger than life hero in a remote time and place. Epic tales were originally handed down orally to explain the myths and legends of a race or country.

Epigraph A motto or quotation that precedes a book or chapter.

Epilogue A concluding section added to the end of a novel or play.

Episodic When a narrative is structured into individual episodes.

Euphemism When one term is substituted as a polite description for a cruder act. i.e. passing instead of dying

Exemplum A short tale or anecdote that serves to teach a moral lesson or exemplify a biblical text.

Fable A brief and simplistic story told for the purpose of highlighting a moral lesson.

First person narrator When the narrative is told through the eyes of one character, using the pronoun 'I'

Genre A category or type of literary work. For example novel, short story, poem etc. Genres can also be more specific – comedy, mystery, love story etc.

The Golden Age According to Greek and Roman Mythology this was the first age of the world. It is described as 'golden' because apparently during this time people were prosperous and peaceful and lived in an ideal state of happiness. A nation may refer to it's own 'golden age' as the period when it was at its peak.

Hyperbole Ridiculously exaggerated language and/or description that is not intended to be taken seriously and is often used for comic effect.

Imagery The use of words to create pictorial images. Imagery often appeals to all the senses of taste, sight, touch and sound and works on both literal and figurative levels.

Intrusive narrator When an omniscient narrator interrupts the flow of the narrative in order to comment upon an event, situation or character.

Irony The discrepancy between the appearance of a situation and its reality. Irony can be verbal – for example when someone says, 'I'm *fine*' but means 'I'm angry'. Or situational – for example a blind man who sells glasses. Dramatic irony is when the audience knows more than the characters.

Juxtapose When one event is positioned alongside another, usually with the intention of creating a literary link between the two. For example the birth of a baby and the simultaneous breaking of a vase.

Metaphorical/Metaphor A figure of speech that ascribes the qualities (literally or imaginatively) of one thing to another. For example 'morning is/a new sheet of paper for you to write on' – Eve Meriam

Narrative method The method in which the author chooses to tell the story.

Narrative point of view The point of view expressed by the narrator.

Narrative strategy The writing strategy or 'game plan' employed by an author. This determines when and how much information is given to the reader about both the characters and the plot.

Narrative structure The way in which the narrative is structured. A story can be told chronologically, using flashbacks, beginning at the end etc.

Narrative styles The different narrative styles an author can use in order to manipulate the reader.

Narrative technique The different methods employed by an author in order to achieve his/her desired affect of the narrative upon the reader.

Omniscient narrator When the narrator has a God-like power of knowing and seeing all action, events and the characters' thoughts.

Parable A short story that contains and illuminates a moral lesson. For example the parable of the tortoise and the hare teaches the moral lesson that slow and steady wins the race.

Pastiche When one art form (drama, musical, literature) consciously mimics another artist's well-known work. This is usually done for satirical purposes. For example Chris Morris's 'Brass Eye' is a pastiche of the genre of news/documentary, typified by TV shows such as 'Panorama.'

Pastoral A pastoral is traditionally a poem that describes various elements of rural life. These verses create an idealised picture of country life usually featuring lovelorn shepherds 'a-wooing' in a field of flowers. As the form evolved, pastoral lyrics, dramas and elegies were also incorporated under the umbrella term of pastoral.

Personification When human characteristics are attributed to plants, animals, inanimate objects or abstract ideas. For example, 'the phone screamed for attention.'

Satire A literary technique that combines many other methods of humour such as sarcasm, wit, irony and caricature in order to create a comic effect. Usually the purpose of the satire is to illuminate the folly, vice or greed of individuals or institutions. For this reason much satire is considered political because it seeks to not only amuse its audience but also to make them realise certain truths about society. Ali G, at the start of his career, was considered a satirist, as he was a Cambridge graduate masquerading as a Staines street youth. He simultaneously managed to make fun of or 'satirise', both youth culture and the establishment's treatment of young 'streetwise' adults.

Symbolise Symbolism is the use of words, characters, actions and objects that are to be understood literally but also represent higher, more abstract concepts. i.e. a caged bird can signify the literal fact of a bird in a cage as well as the symbolic values of lost freedom, feeling trapped etc.

Third person When a narrator tells the story from outside the narrative, yet also from a characters' perspective. i.e. 'Millie sat down weakly and thought "Well that's it then" '.

Tone The attitude of the writing – be it carefree, formal, suspenseful etc.

Tragedy A piece of fiction that traces the downfall of a protagonist who is often portrayed as being 'better' than the rest of us. The 'tragedy' is that the fall from grace is brought about through some accident, an error in judgement or a cruel twist of fate. Often it occurs because of a 'tragic flaw' within the protagonist.

Travesty A grotesque version of Burlesque (see above)

Trilogy Any three literary or musical works that are thematically linked. For example the Greek tragedies *Oedipus Rex*, *Oedipus at Colonus* and *Antigone*

Tropes Figures of speech

Unreliable narrator When a reader feels they cannot entirely trust their narrator.

Biographical outline

1954 Louis de Bernières born in London.

1977 Graduated in Philosophy from Manchester University.

1982 Left teaching at a school in Ipswich to write.

1990 *The War of Don Emmanuel's Nether Parts* published.

1991 *Señor Vivo and the Coca Lord* published. Won the Commonwealth Writers' Prize Best First Book Eurasia Region for *The War of Don Emmanuel's Nether Parts*.

1992 *The Troublesome Offspring of Cardinal Guzman* published. Won the Commonwealth Writers' Prize Best Book Eurasia Region for *Señor Vivo and the Coca Lord*.

1993 Chosen as one of the 20 Best of Young British Novelists.

1994 *Captain Corelli's Mandolin* published and shortlisted for *Sunday Express* Book of the Year.

1995 Won the Commonwealth Writers' Prize Best Book for *Captain Corelli's Mandolin*.

2001 Film of *Captain Corelli's Mandolin* released. *Red Dog* published.

Select bibliography

WORKS BY LOUIS DE BERNIÈRES

The War of Don Emmanuel's Nether Parts (Secker and Warburg, 1990; Vintage, 1991)

Señor Vivo and the Coca Lord (Secker and Warburg, 1991; Vintage, 1992)

The Troublesome Offspring of Cardinal Guzman (Secker and Warburg, 1992; Vintage, 1993)

Captain Corelli's Mandolin (Secker and Warburg, 1994; Vintage, 1995)

Sunday Morning at the Centre of the World (Vintage 2001)

Red Dog (Secker and Warburg, 2001; Vintage, 2002)

Shawn Slovo, *Captain Corelli Film Script* (Vintage, 2001)

CRITICAL WORKS

Jose Arroyo, 'Paradise Lust' *Sight and Sound* May 2001, Vol. 11 no. 5 pp. 16–18

Emily A McDermott, 'Every Man's an Odysseus: An Analysis of the Nostos Theme in Corelli's Mandolin' *Classical and Modern Literature: A Quarterly* (Winter 2000), Vol. 20 no. 2 pp. 21–37

Sascha Talmor, 'An Englishman in Latin America: The War of Don Emmanuel's Nether Parts' *History of European Ideas* (January 1993), vol. 17 no. 1 pp. 73–94

Also available in Vintage

Louis de Bernières

RED DOG

'In early 1998 I went to Perth in Western Australia in order to attend the literature festival, and part of the arrangement was that I should go to Karratha to do their first ever literary dinner. Karratha is a mining town a long way further north. The landscape is extraordinary, being composed of vast heaps of dark red earth and rock poking out of the never-ending bush. I imagine that Mars must have a similar feel to it.

'I went exploring and discovered the bronze statue to Red Dog outside the town of Dampier. I felt straight away that I had to find out more about this splendid dog.

'A few months later I returned to Western Australia and spent two glorious weeks driving around collecting Red Dog stories and visiting the places that he knew, writing up the text as I went along. I hope my cat never finds out that I have written a story to celebrate the life of a dog.'

'When I finished the final chapter I immediately extended a sought-after invitation to my dog to spend the night on the bed. It is that sort of book. If you love Australia it will have you aching for the scent of gums and sight of the Southern Cross, while if you love dogs it is sure to make you highly indulgent to the one you love'
Observer

'Will this become another word-of-mouth *Corelli*-style bestseller? It is certainly possible . . . life enhancing reading'
Literary Review

'De Bernières brilliantly evokes the red heat of Australian summers. Heat lifts off the pages: turning them is like opening furnace doors'
Spectator

Also available in Vintage Living Texts

Sebastian Faulks

Focusing on:
Birdsong
The Girl at the Lion d'Or
Charlotte Gray

In **Vintage Living Texts**, teachers and students will find the essential guide to the works of Sebastian Faulks. **Vintage Living Texts** is unique in that it offers an in-depth interview with Sebastian Faulks, relating specifically to the texts under discussion.

This guide deals with Faulks's themes, genre and narrative technique, and a close reading of the texts will provide a rich source of ideas for intelligent and inventive ways of approaching the novels.

Also included in this guide are detailed reading plans for all three novels, questions for essays and discussion, contextual material, suggested texts for complementary and comparative reading, extracts from reviews, a biography, bibliography, reading list of literary criticism and a glossary of literary terms.

Whether a teacher, student or general reader, **Vintage Living Texts** give you the chance to explore new resources and enjoy new pleasures.

Also available in Vintage Living Texts

Ian McEwan

Focusing on:
Enduring Love
The Child in Time
Atonement

In **Vintage Living Texts**, teachers and students will find the essential guide to the works of Ian McEwan. **Vintage Living Texts** is unique in that it offers an in-depth interview with Ian McEwan, relating specifically to the texts under discussion.

This guide deals with McEwan's themes, genre and narrative technique, and a close reading of the texts will provide a rich source of ideas for intelligent and inventive ways of approaching the novels.

Also included in this guide are detailed reading plans for all three novels, questions for essays and discussion, contextual material, suggested texts for complementary and comparative reading, extracts from reviews, a biography, bibliography, reading list of literary criticism and a glossary of literary terms.

Whether a teacher, student or general reader, **Vintage Living Texts** give you the chance to explore new resources and enjoy new pleasures.

Also available in Vintage Living Texts

Margaret Atwood

Focusing on:
The Handmaid's Tale
The Blind Assassin
Bluebeard's Egg and other Stories

In **Vintage Living Texts**, teachers and students will find the essential guide to the works of Margaret Atwood. **Vintage Living Texts** is unique in that it offers an in-depth interview with Margaret Atwood, relating specifically to the texts under discussion.

This guide deals with Atwood's themes, genre and narrative technique, and a close reading of the texts will provide a rich source of ideas for intelligent and inventive ways of approaching the novels.

Also included in this guide are detailed reading plans for all three novels, questions for essays and discussion, contextual material, suggested texts for complementary and comparative reading, extracts from reviews, a biography, bibliography, reading list of literary criticism and a glossary of literary terms.

Whether a teacher, student or general reader, **Vintage Living Texts** give you the chance to explore new resources and enjoy new pleasures.

BY LOUIS DE BERNIÈRES
ALSO AVAILABLE IN VINTAGE